BIG STUFF IN THE MARITIMES

BOOK # 3

Katherine E. Tapley-Milton

PUBLISHED BY

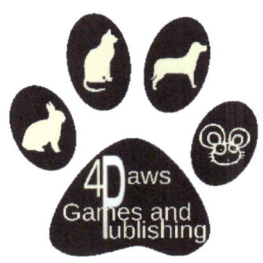

BRUNO, SASKATCHEWAN, CANADA

Big Stuff in the Maritimes, Book # 3

Written and Created by Katherine E. Tapley-Milton

Photos by Katherine E. Tapley-Milton

Cover Art by 4 Paws Games and Publishing

Edited by Kathrine E. Tapley-Milton and 4 Paws Games and Publishing

Formatted and Published by 4 Paws Games and Publishing
Published May 2018 First Edition
 ISBN-13: 978-1988345826
ISBN-10: 1988345820

Copyright © 2018 by Katherine E. Tapley-Milton
All Rights Reserved
Published by 4 Paws Games and Publishing
P.O. Box 444
Humboldt, Saskatchewan, Canada S0K 2A0
http://www.4-Paws-Games-and-Publishing.ca
Publishing logo and name copyright © 2016
All Rights Reserved

The publisher is not responsible for the book, website, or social media (or its content) that is not owned by the publisher. All legal matters are to be taken up by the author as the publisher holds no responsibilities.

The author and publisher have made every effort to ensure the accuracy of the information within this book was correct at time of publication. The author and publisher acknowledge that not every location is in the book at this time.

No part of this publication may be reproduced, distributed, or transmitted in any form or by any means, including photocopying, recording, or other electronic or mechanical methods, without the prior written permission of the publisher, except in the case of brief quotations embodied in critical reviews and certain other non-commercial uses permitted by copyright law.

Attention: Permission C/O
Katherine E. Tapley-Milton
18 Squire Street
Sackville, New Brunswick E4L 4K9

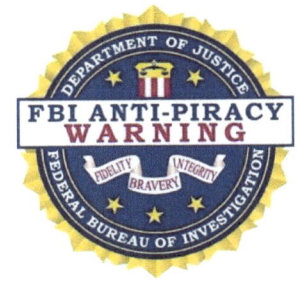

Other Books by Katherine E. Tapley-Milton

Big Stuff in the Maritimes Series
1-3

Other Books
Kathy's Down East Christmas Cookbook
Mother Tapley's Recipe Book: Tasty Down East Cooking
The Disappearing Mailboxes of New Brunswick and Nova Scotia: A Touring of Mailboxes
Old Boats and Old Quotes
The Adventures of the Three Mouse-Breath-Kateers
The Adventures of Sir Lancelot the Cat
Scintillating Scarecrows
And more.

Find Katherine Online
Website
http://authorkatherinetapleymilton.weebly.com

Facebook
https://www.facebook.com/KatherineETapleyMilton

Amazon Authors Central Page
https://www.amazon.com/Katherine-Tapley-Milton/e/B00CP8EBR8

Like the book? Please post a review online where you bought it!

TABLE OF CONTENTS

PREFACE 1
NEW BRUNSWICK 2
  MAUGERVILLE 2
    THE ADIRONDACK CHAIR 3
  MONCTON 4
    NORTHROP FRYE 5
  PENOBSQUIS 6
    ANIMALAND CAMPGROUND 19
  SACKVILLE 20
    DR. GEORGE FRANCIS GILLMAN STANLEY 21
NOVA SCOTIA 22
  AMHERST 22
    VICTORIAN LADY 23
  AMHERST 24
    THE BAG PIPER STATUE 25
  BEDFORD 26
    GIANT SUNFLOWER 27
  CHÉVERIE 28
    THE CAMERA OBSCURA 29
  FIVE ISLANDS 30
    THE MYSTERY OF THE MARY CELESTE 31
  HALIFAX 32

- THE RAT PACK 33
- HALIFAX 34
  - THE WAVE 35
- PARRSBORO 36
  - T-REX DEFENDS ROCK, MINERAL AND FOSSIL SHOP 37
- TURO 38
  - GIANT HOCKEY STICK AS A TRIBUTE 41
- PRINCE EDWARD ISLAND 42
  - CAPE EGMONT 42
    - MESSAGE IN A BOTTLE 49
  - CAVENDISH 50
    - SHARK HEAD ON A ROOF 51
  - LAURETTE 52
    - THE LARGEST WOVEN BASKET ON PEI 53
  - O'LEARY 54
    - POTATO MUSEUM 55
  - SUMMERSIDE 56
    - BERNIE, THE TRAVELLER 57
- ABOUT KATHERINE E. TAPLEY-MILTON 58

PREFACE

I have been working on "Big Stuff in the Maritimes" for many years now. Every time we took a vacation in the Maritimes, I was delighted to photograph some folk-art statues, just for fun and my own personal use. There have been any magazine articles done on some of the statues, but there aren't many books specifically for the Maritime provinces. I used "Large Canadian Roadside Attractions" in my research. However, I mainly utilized lists found in: "Big Things in Nova Scotia;" "Big Things in New Brunswick;" and "Big Things in Prince Edward Island" as maps for my photography. I also consulted the following list of statues that were extremely helpful: http://www.bigthings.ca/bignb.html

http://www.bigthings.ca/bigns.html; and http://www.bigthings.ca/bigpei.html.

Finally, I could not have done this book without the help of my husband, Dave, who drove me around and did some backup photos for me. He is an indispensable part of this book. In the process of photographing and researching, "Big Stuff in the Maritimes," I came to know the Maritime provinces much better and learned a lot of history as well.

NEW BRUNSWICK
MAUGERVILLE

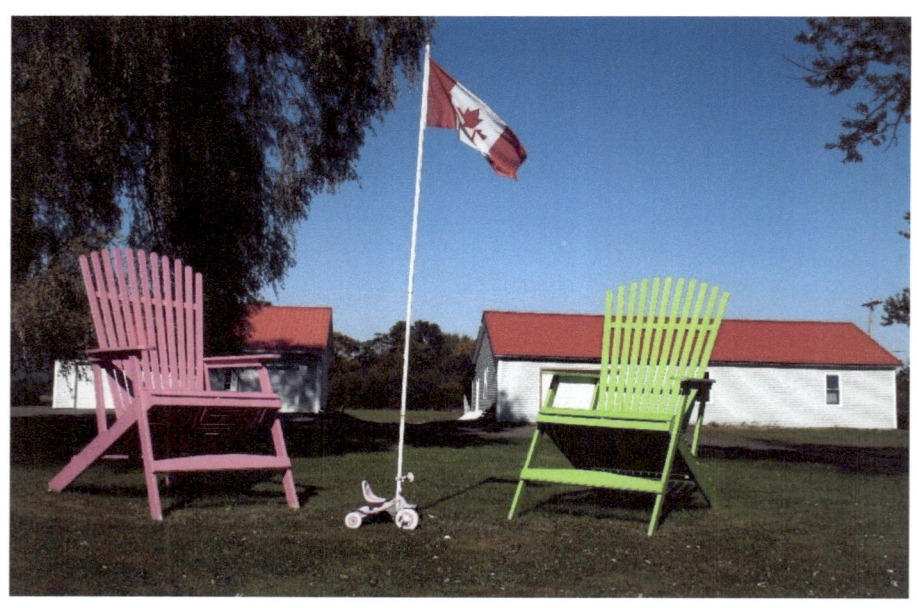

THE ADIRONDACK CHAIR

It is getting popular today to make oversized Adirondack chair and set them on lawns or by beaches. There are two such chairs on a lawn in Maugerville, New Brunswick.

Thomas Lee invented this kind of chair and had a big family of twenty-two, so he had lots of help trying out his new type of furniture.

"The first Adirondack chair was created by (him) around 1903. Lee was searching in vain for comfortable outdoor furniture for his country cottage in Westport, NY, which is near the Adirondack mountain region of upstate New York, on the banks of Lake Champlain." [1]

---

[1] http://www.apartmenttherapy.com/adirondack-chairs-quick-histor-118981

MONCTON

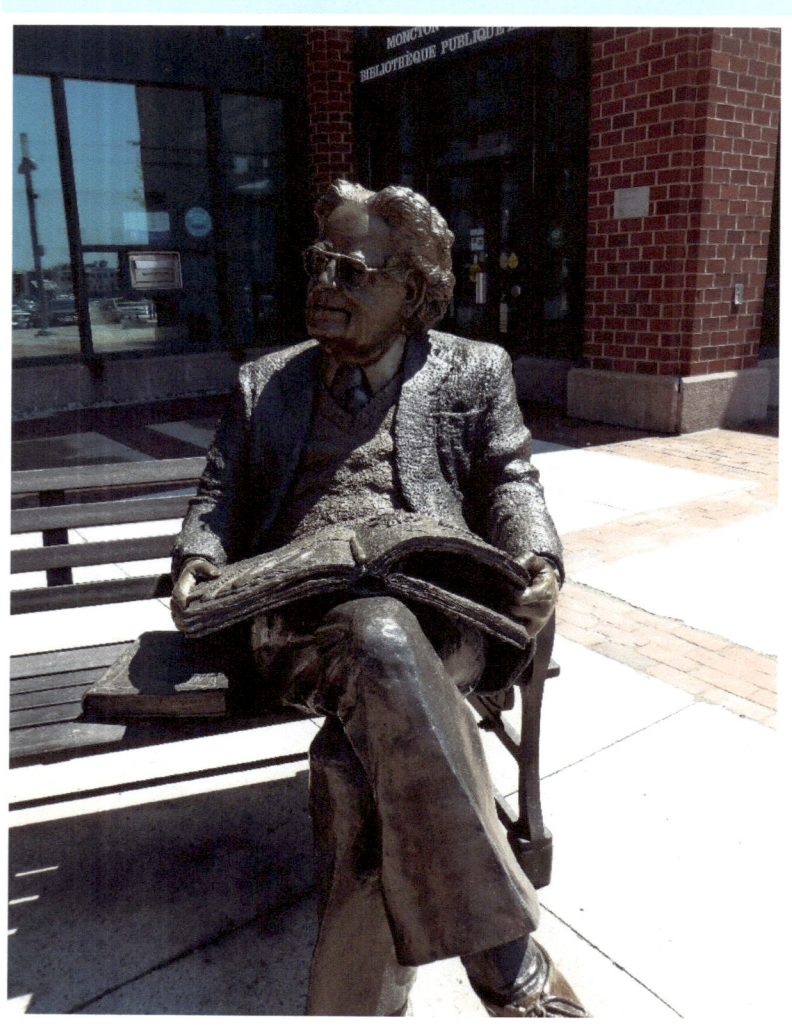

NORTHROP FRYE

Northrop Frye was a famous intellectual, prolific writer, and United Church Minister who wrote over twenty books. His most famous book was written in 1957 and titled, "The Anatomy of Criticism".

Frye was born on July 14th, 1912 in Sherbrook, Quebec. When he was seven years old his family moved to Moncton, New Brunswick. In 1929, Northrop won a typing contest and went to Toronto to study philosophy and theology. He was to spend most of his life in Toronto.

Northrop got his Masters in English from Oxford University and received first class honors. He died on January 23, 1991. During his lifetime he lectured at over 100 universities worldwide and held 30 honorary degrees.

Every summer Moncton holds a Northrop Frye Festival to encourage writers and poets. There are workshops, creative exercises, and readings. It lasts for a week.

PENOBSQUIS

Pictures in order:

1. The Animaland Campground sign.
2. Blue duck.
3. Bowling ball.
4. Elephant.
5. Giraffe.
6. Lobster slide.
7. Mushroom.
8. Octopus slide.
9. Snail.
10. Whale.
11. Yellow bird.
12. Albino moose.

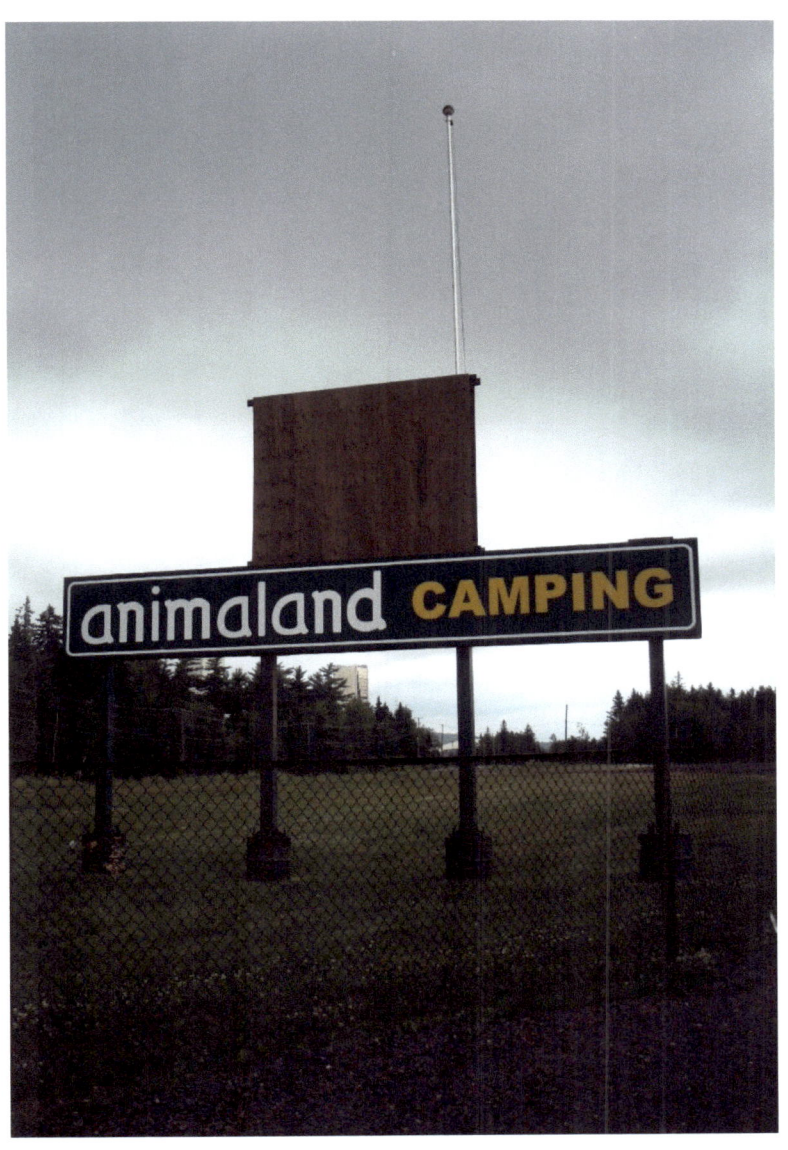

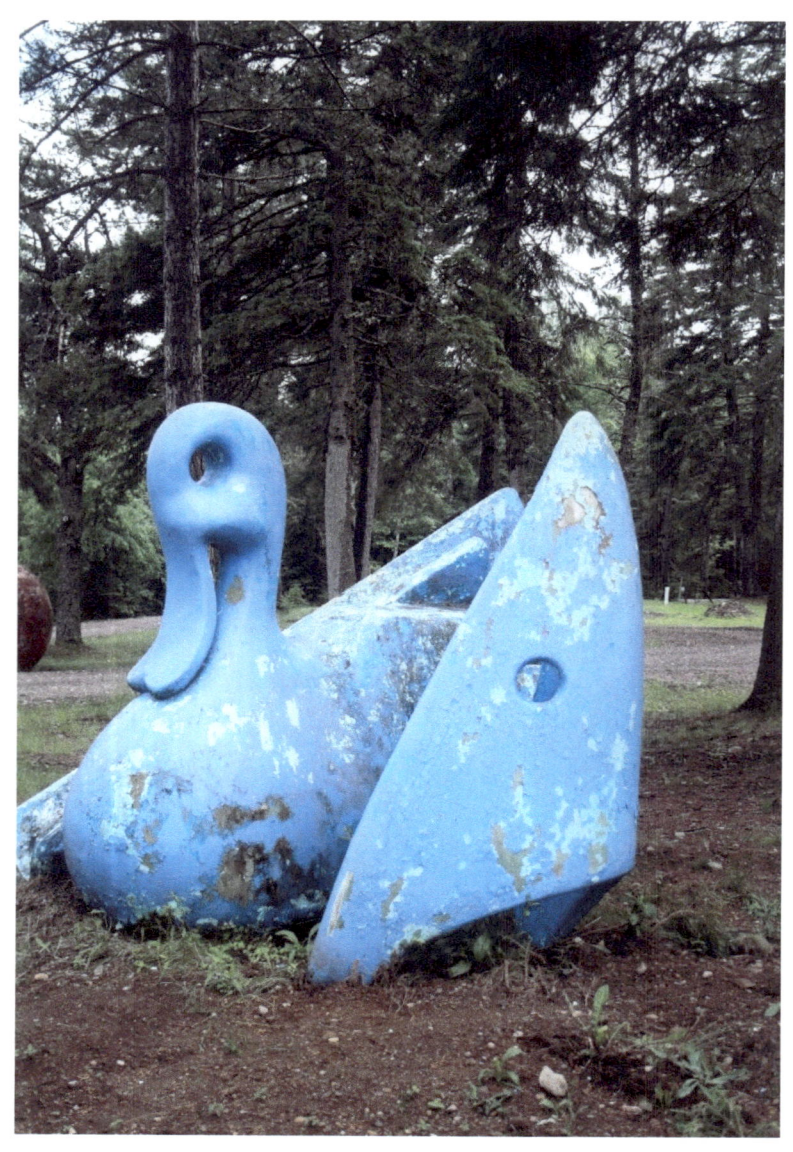

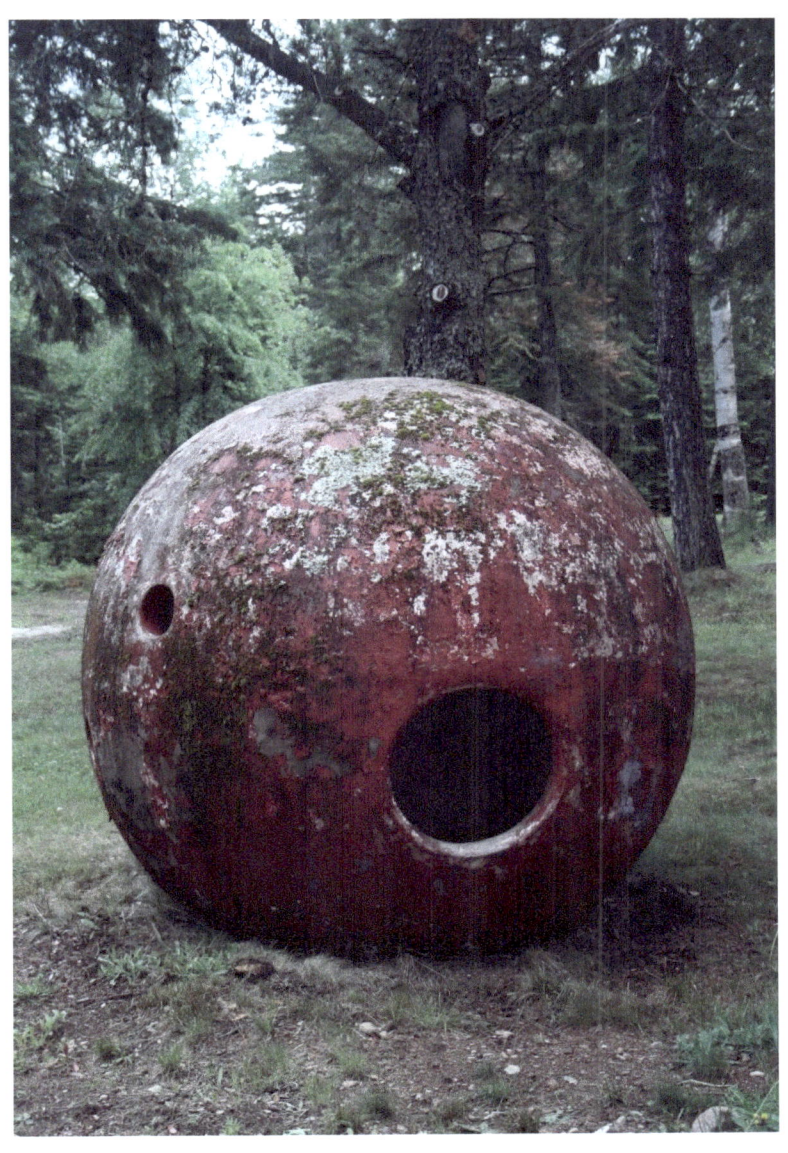

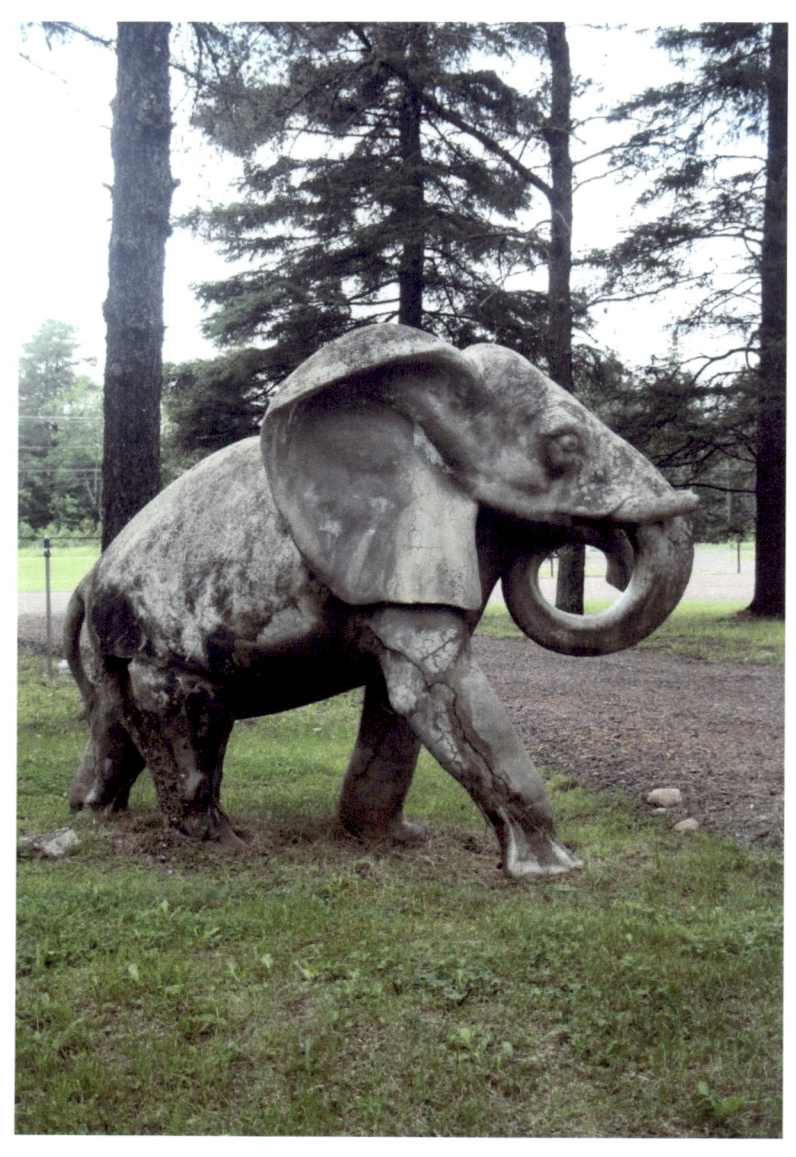

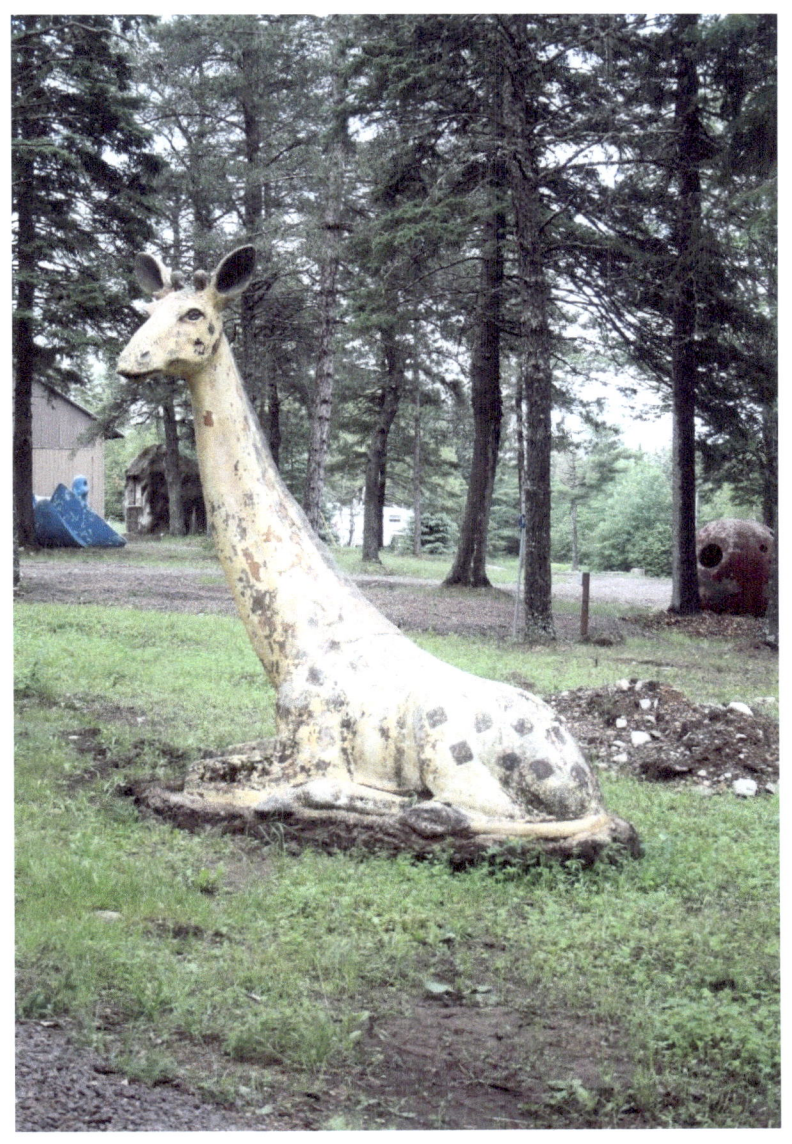

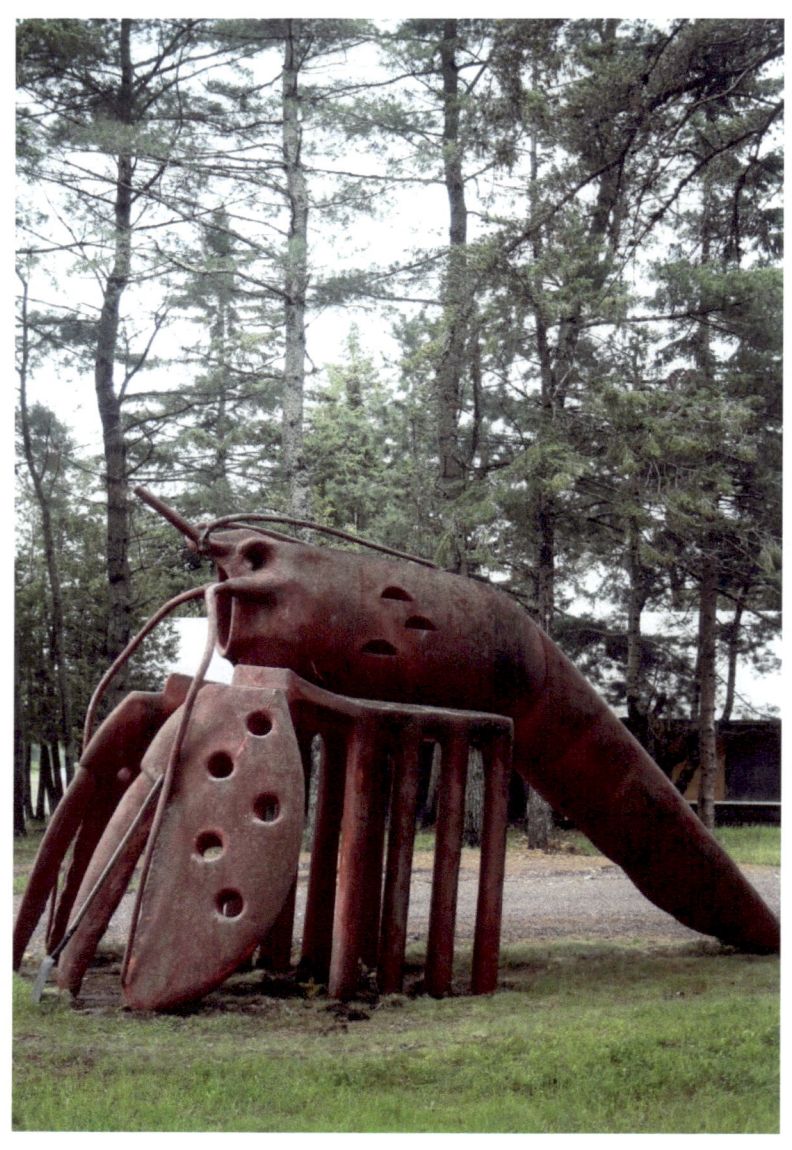

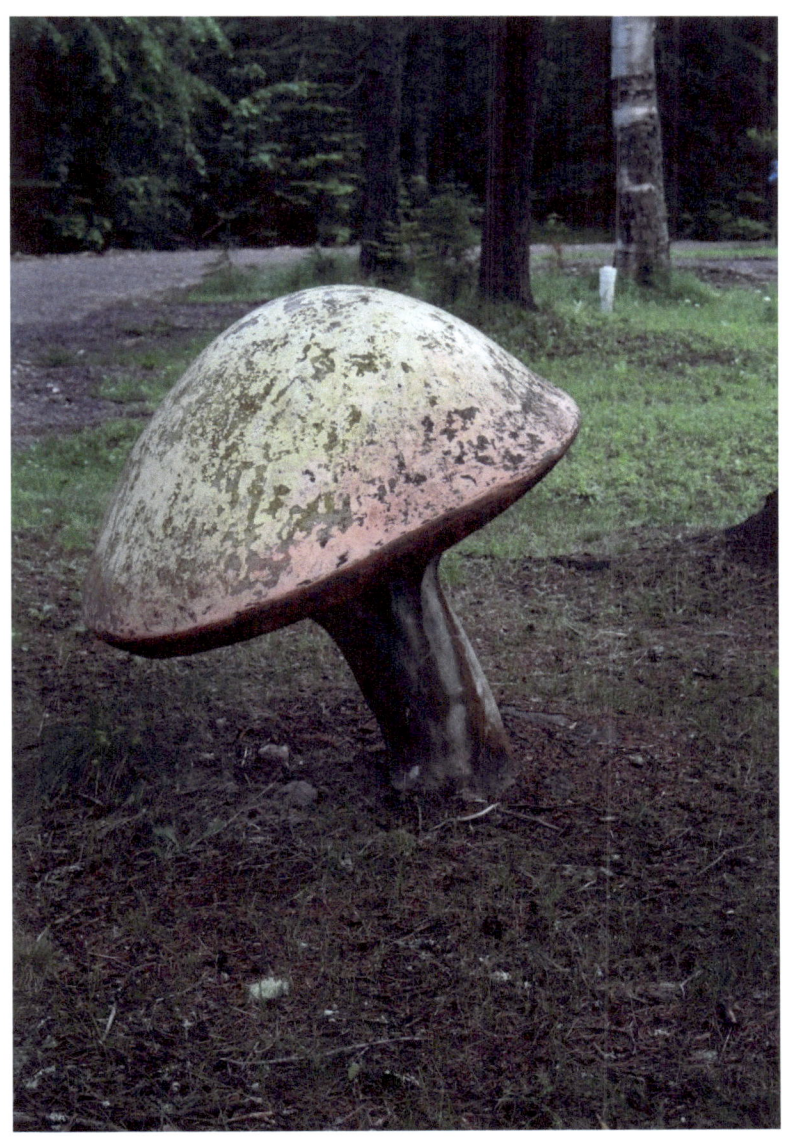

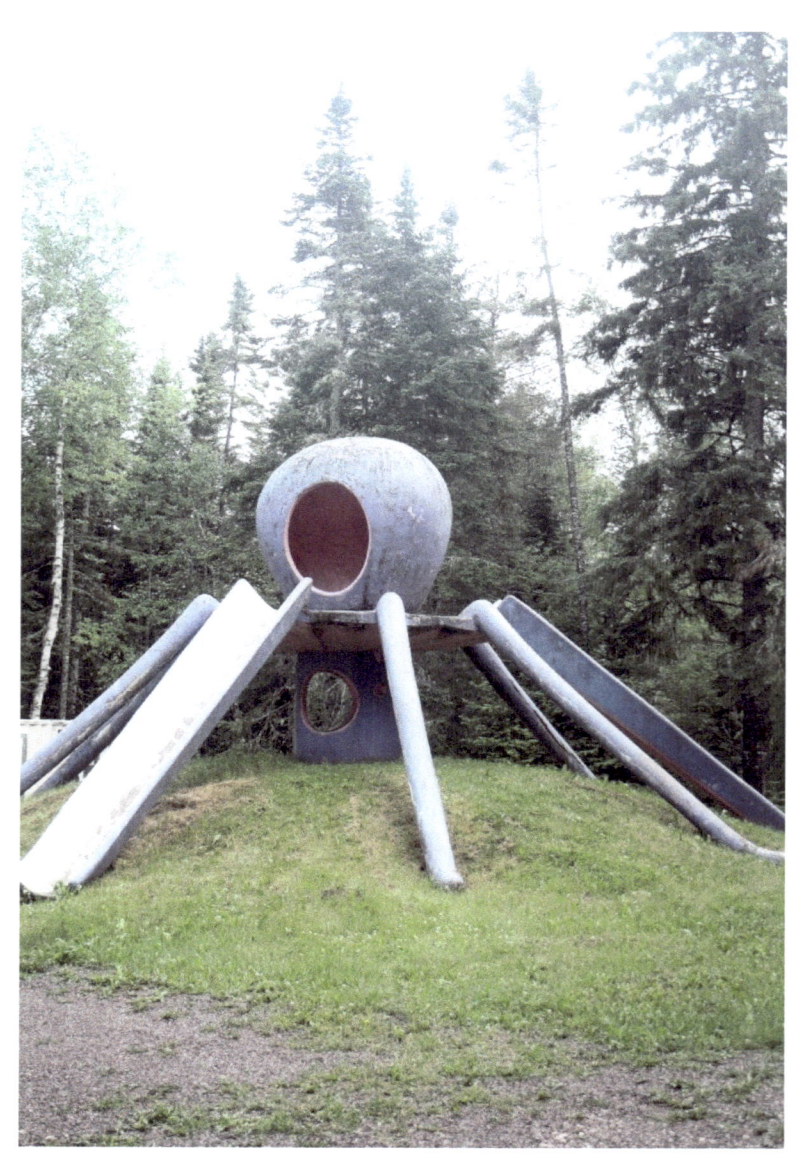

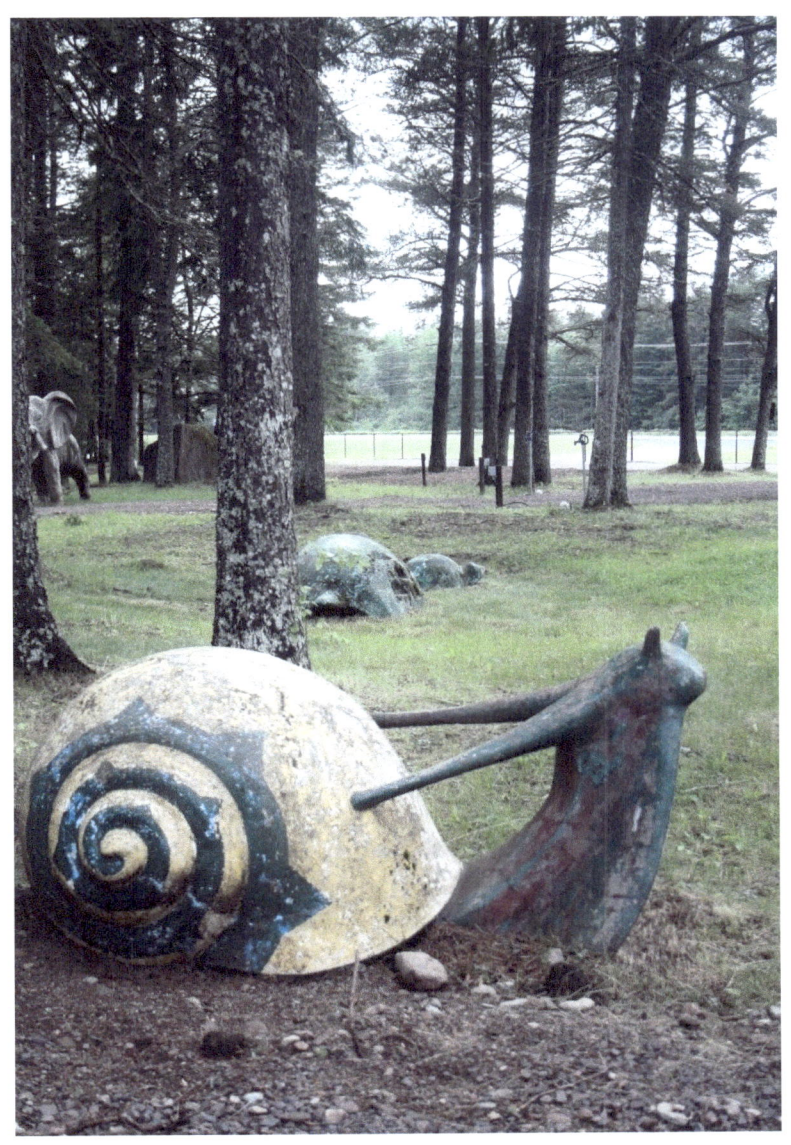

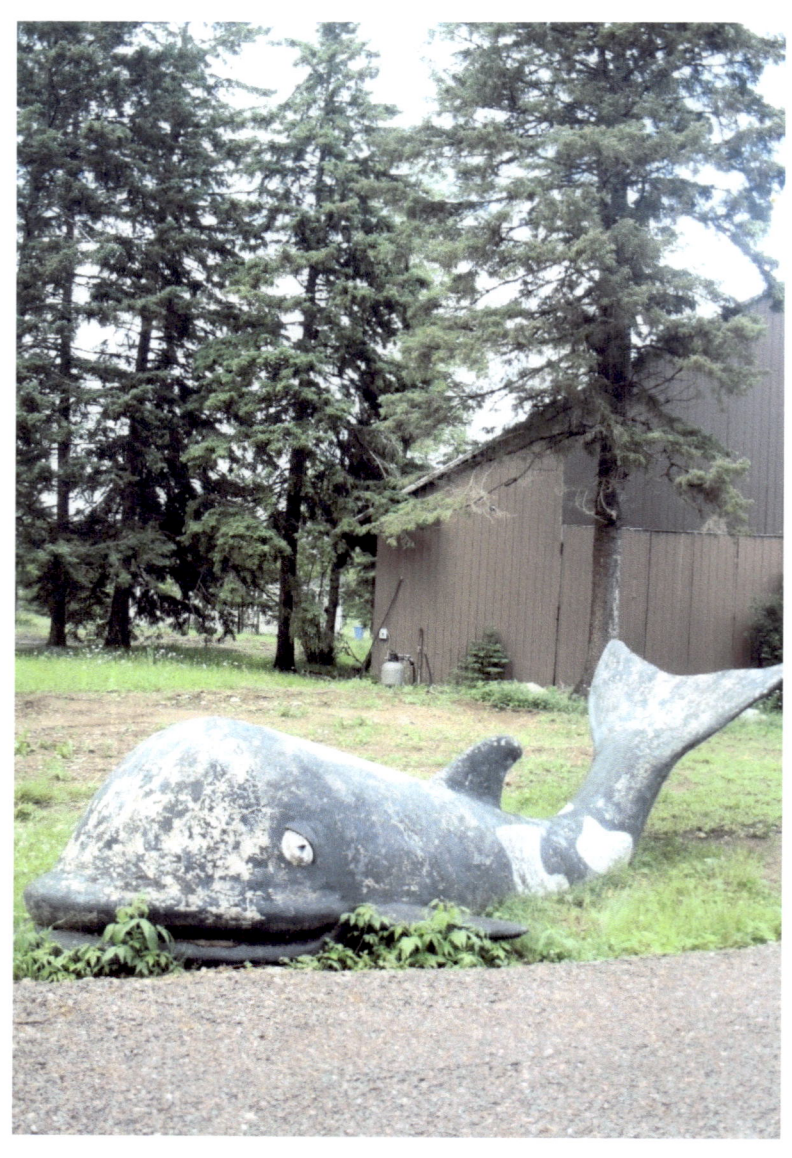

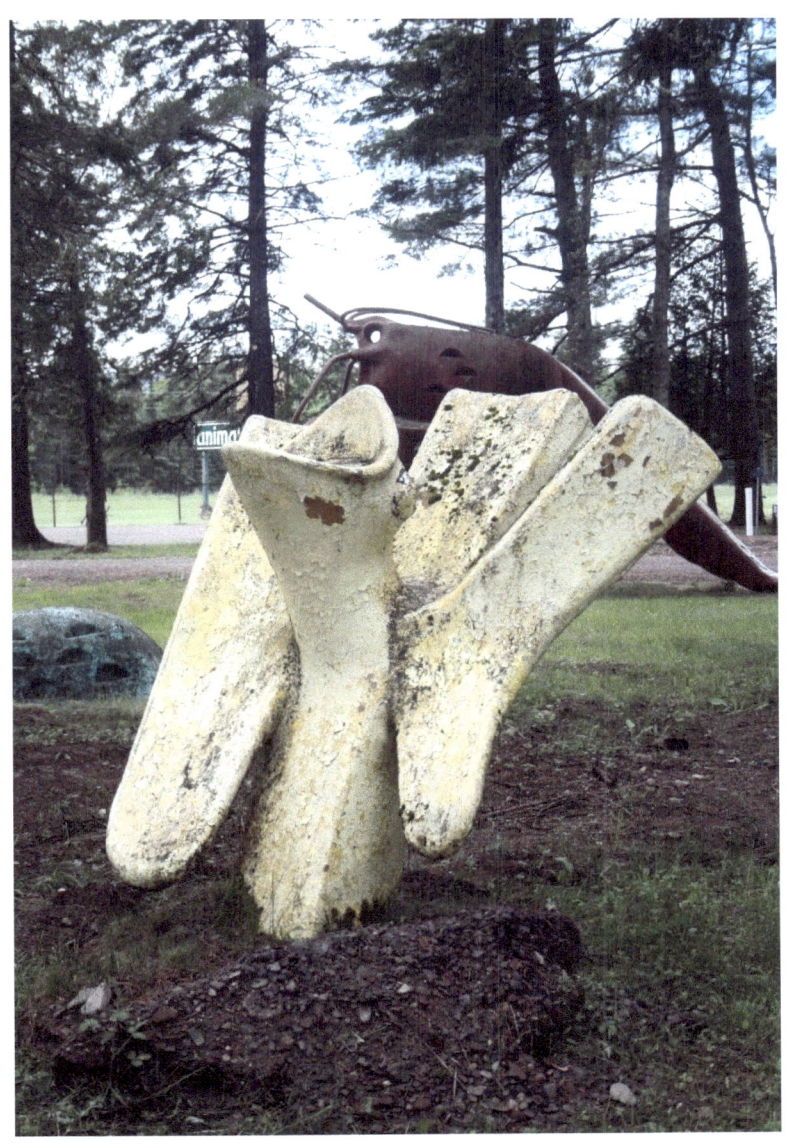

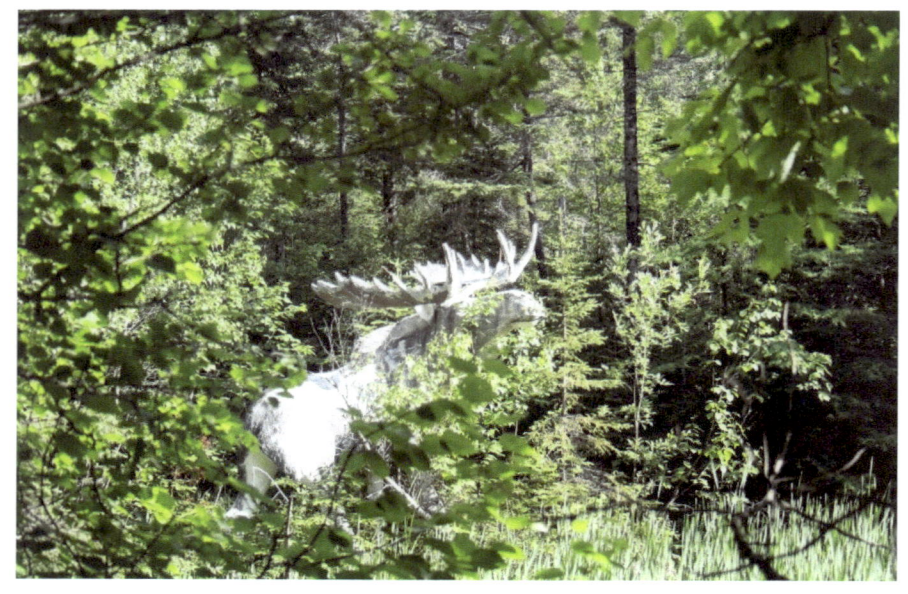

ANIMALAND CAMPGROUND

In Penobsquis, New Brunswick, on Route114, there is a child's amusement park that was created by Winston Atwood Bronum. It is called "Animaland" and was popular in the 1970's and 1980's. It is now a campground, but there still is a giraffe, an elephant, a snail, a lobster slide, an octopus slide, a whale, fighting moose and bear statues in the bushes, and "Blowhard" the Racehorse, all who are suffering the ravages of time.

Bronum also created the large lobster statue in Shediac, NB and the big potato in Maugerville, NB, but his home base was a cabin in the heart of Animaland. Bronum was born in 1929 and died in 1991. When he was young, he worked on building bridges and hydro dams, which gave him experience in creating large structures. However, it was Bronum artistic skills that made his statues lifelike. Starting in June 2016, Ulie Fournier has made Animaland into a campground and has plans to paint Animaland's statues and generally fix up the dilapidated remains of Bronum's work.

SACKVILLE

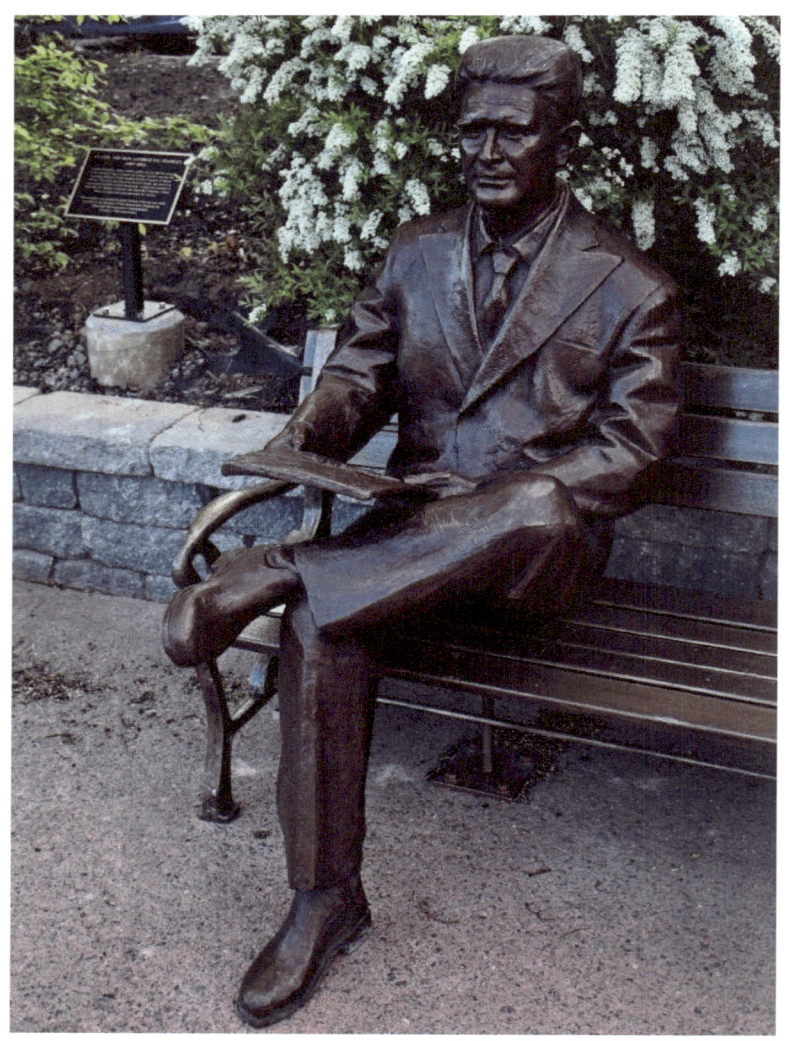

DR. GEORGE FRANCIS GILLMAN STANLEY

Dr. G. F. G. Stanley had an illustrious career as a professor, military man, a historian, prolific author, and designer of the Canadian flag. He acted as an administrator at Mount Allison University from 1936-40 and 1969-75. From 1982-87 Dr. Stanley served as Lieutenant-governor of New Brunswick and in 1995 was awarded the Order of Canada.

He had a life long interest in Louis Riel and wrote a thought provoking biography of him. Some of his other books are "The War of 1812"; "Canada's Soldiers"; "Canada Invaded: 1775-76"; "Battle in the Dark: Stoney Creek"; and "The Birth of Western Canada".

Dr. Stanley and his wife, Ruth, were long time residents of Sackville, New Brunswick. They had three girls – Marietta, Della, and Laurie, who all went on to have notable careers themselves. A sitting statue of Dr. Stanley can be found in the middle of Sackville, near the post office.

NOVA SCOTIA

AMHERST

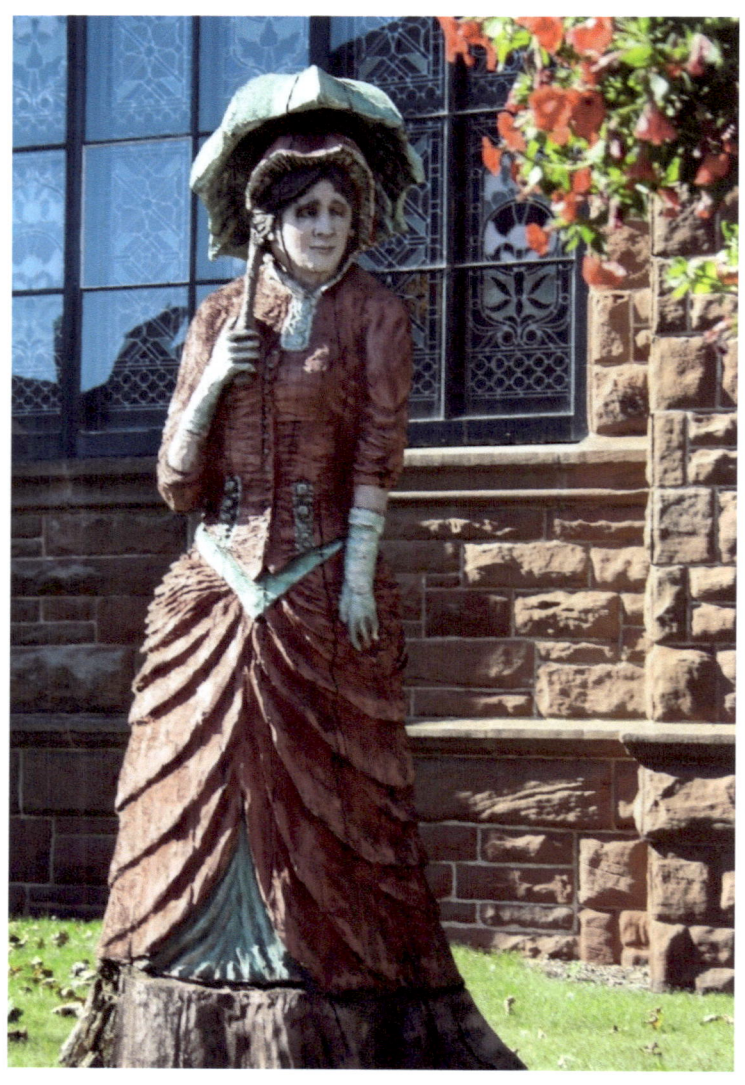

VICTORIAN LADY

In Amherst, Nova Scotia's Victoria Park stands an elegantly dressed Victorian lady carved by Bruce Hebert. She stands 10 feet tall and was carved out of an ailing Elm tree. The lady gives a certain "Old World" charm to downtown Amherst.

AMHERST

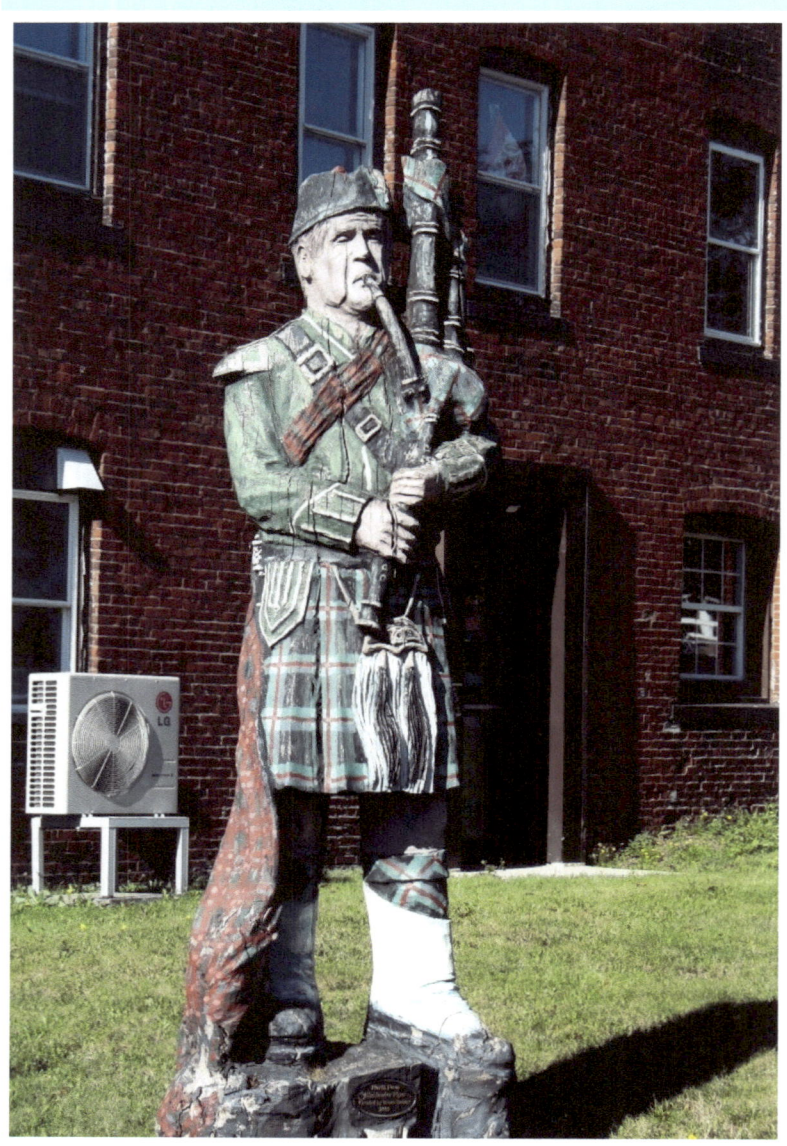

THE BAG PIPER STATUE

In Amherst, Nova Scotia, there is a bag piper statue in Victoria Park. It was carved by Paul Hebert out of an elm tree that was destroyed by Dutch Elm Disease. The statue stands 3.5 metres (11-1/2 feet) tall and is a proud symbol of Nova Scotia's Scottish heritage. In former days there used to be a live bag piper who stood on the Nova Scotia/New Brunswick border and played the pipes for tourists.

BEDFORD

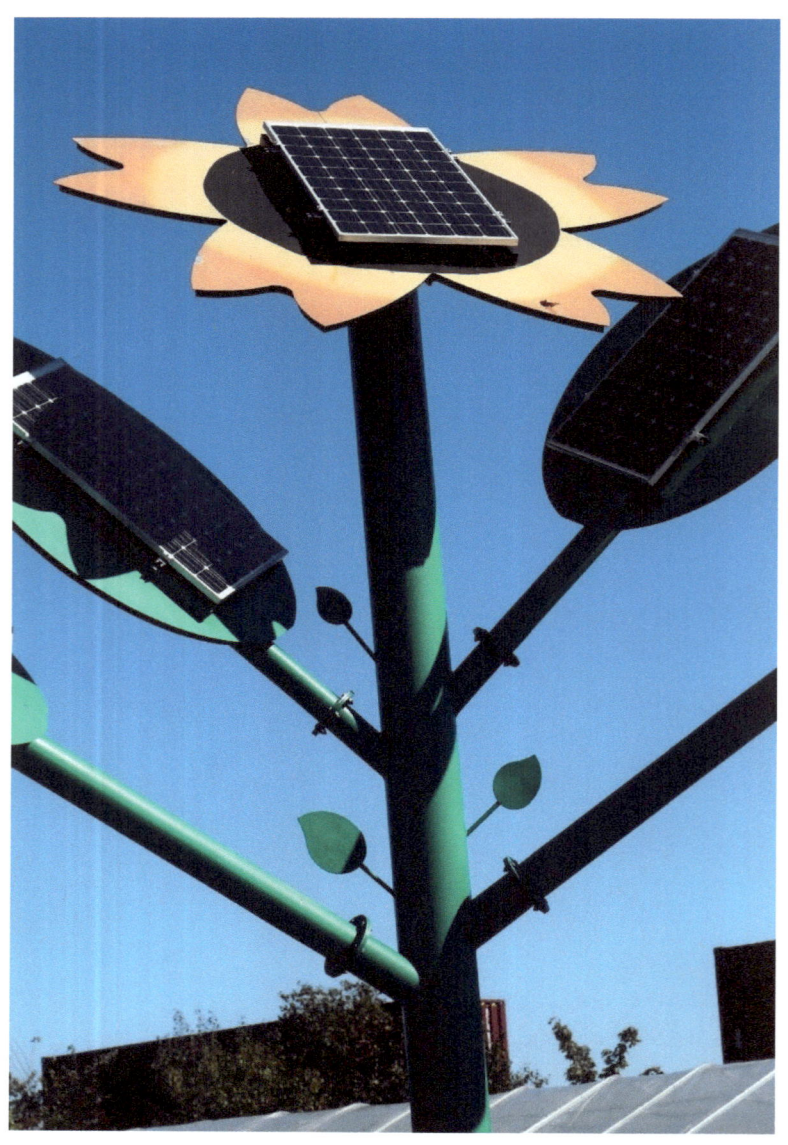

GIANT SUNFLOWER

When Stephen Weagle and his wife were thinking about promoting their solar power business, the idea of building a giant sunflower with solar panels came to them. Weagle comments, "Sunflowers are actually the most efficient design in nature for the collection of sun ..." [2]

His company name is *Sunflower Solar Inc.* and he says that the demand for solar power is increasing. The giant sunflower has 245-watt solar panels and batteries to store the sun's power on it's leaves and blossom. Surrounding businesses benefit by getting their power and light for free. Weagle says that the sunflower is in an excellent place to collect the sun's rays. He comments that if you install solar energy you may get 40 years of power without any maintenance. Certainly, Weagle's giant statue of a sunflower grabs one's attention. The sunflower can be seen on the Bedford, Nova Scotia highway.

---

[2] http://www.novanewsnow.com/news/regional/sunflower-power-solar-flower-blooms-on-bedford-highway-84382

CHÉVERIE

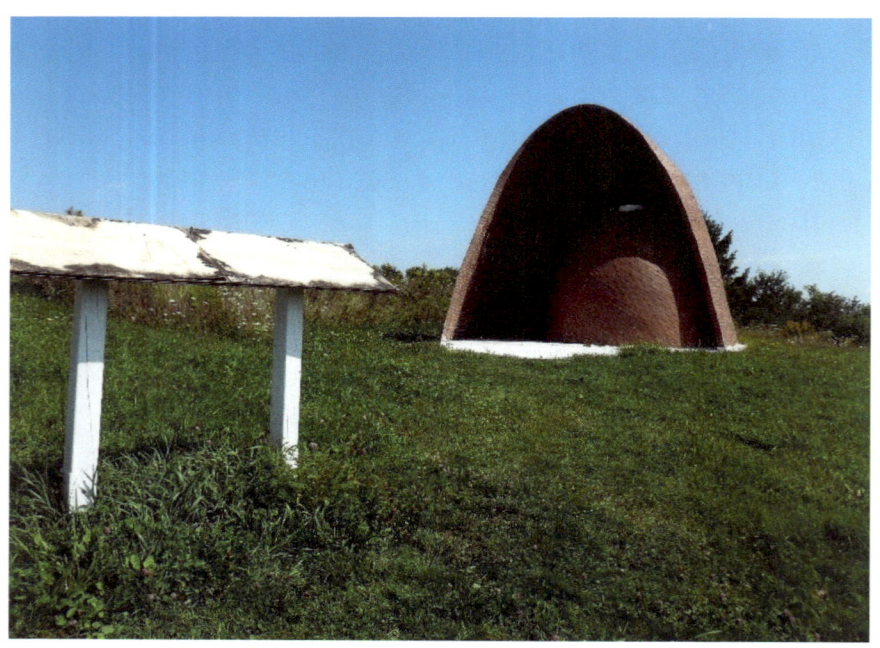

THE CAMERA OBSCURA

In Cheverie, Nova Scotia there is an unusual sight in a field by the ocean. It is a camera obscura which works like a giant pin hole camera. Dalhousie University's Coastal Studio comments, "This parabolic brickshell frames the tidal landscape, acting as a camera obscura, a device which records the rising tides of the salt marsh at the mouth of the river. The pavilion utilizes the layering of brick tiles to create three outer arch-shaped, self-supporting walls and an indoor oval-shaped room that shelters the camera obscura. The camera obscura is found as a darkened room with a small mirror on an outside wall. As light from the exterior passes through the small opening, the tidal scene is projected, upside down, onto the interior floor."

It is well worth the drive to see this unusual camera and to go to the nearby beach. Graduate students at Dalhousie University built the camera and it should stand for many years to come.

FIVE ISLANDS

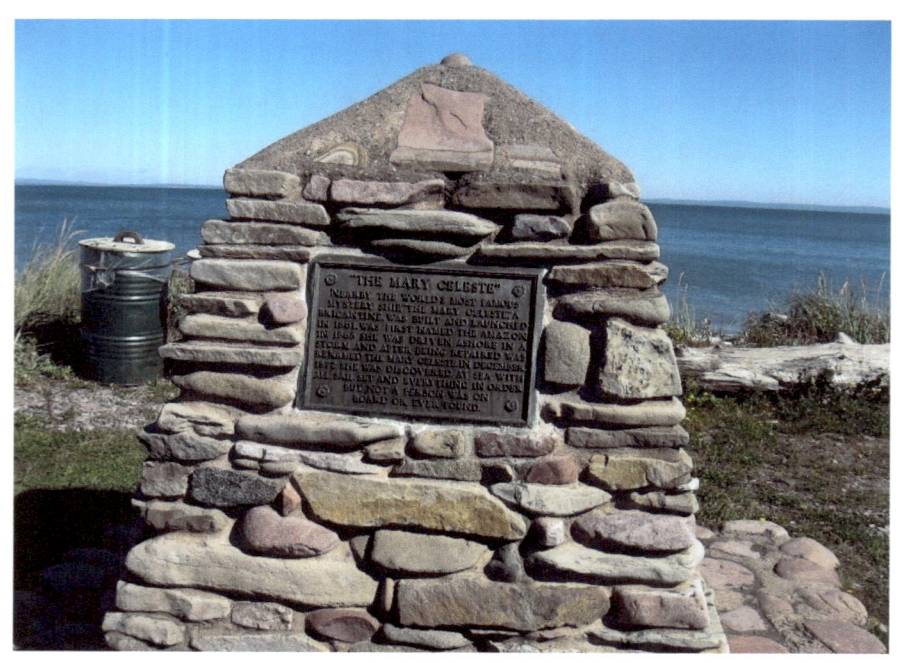

THE MYSTERY OF THE MARY CELESTE

This cairn can be found at Five Islands, Nova Scotia. It commemorates the ship, the *Mary Celeste*. It was a 282-ton brigantine that set sail on November 7th, 1872 from New York and its destination was Genoa, Italy. On the ship were eight crew members, the captain, his wife, and their two-year-old child.[3]

Less than a month later the Mary Celeste was found on December 5th, 400 miles east of the Azores. It was at full sail and nobody was on the ship. The vessel was intact and there wasn't any evidence of piracy or foul play. The Mary Celeste was carrying 1,700 barrels of crude alcohol and there were enough provisions to last six months.

One of the life boats was missing, but that doesn't answer the questions as to why the captain would have ordered the crew to abandon ship or what happened to them. Many theories abound about the Mary Celeste, but it remains an unsolved mystery. [4]

---

[4] http://www.history.com/news/askhistory/what-happened-to-the-mary-celeste

HALIFAX

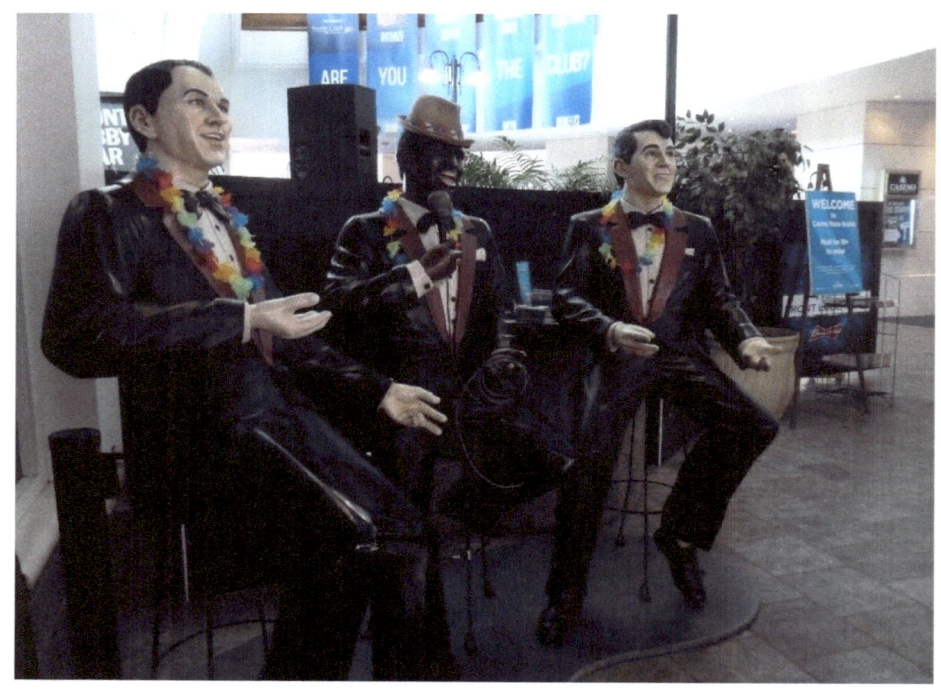

THE RAT PACK

In the entrance, the Halifax Casino has life sized statues of "The Rat Pack;" which consisted of Dean Martin, Sammy Davis Jr., Frank Sinatra, and Peter Lawford. It is not quite certain how the four got their nick name and sometimes other entertainers were satellite members of the Rat Pack.

Wikipedia comments, "The **Rat Pack** is a term used by the media to refer to an informal group of entertainers centered on the Las Vegas casino scene. Having its origins in a group of friends that met at the Los Angeles home of Humphrey Bogart and Lauren Bacall, ..." [5]

All of the members entertained in the 1960's.

---

[5] https://en.wikipedia.org/wiki/Rat_Pack

HALIFAX

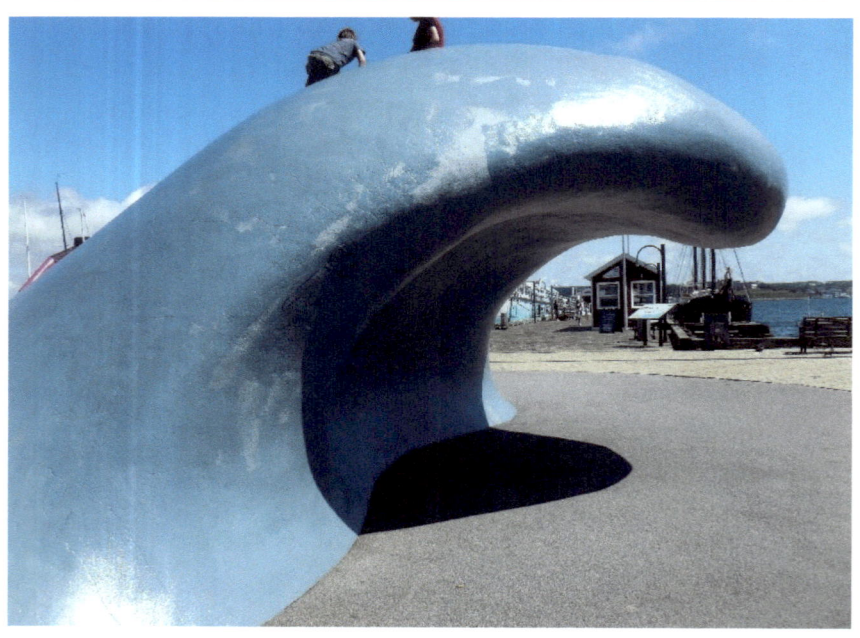

THE WAVE

In 1988, the city of Halifax commissioned a sculpture for the waterfront. The world-class artist, Alex Colville, was among the judges that evaluated artists' proposals. Halifax artist, Donna Hiebert won the bid to make a statue. She constructed, "The Wave," which is a 3.6 metre sculpture constructed out of ferroconcrete. It has a sandy texture, but the paint makes it smooth.

From the beginning there had been concerns for the safety of children climbing on it and the litigation that might ensue. However, in the end the city of Halifax put some foam around "The Wave" so that children will have a soft landing, when they jump off it.

Writing in the "Chronical Herald" December 18, 2013 Hillary Beaumont quoted, Hiebert as commenting: "My impression is that a whole generation, at least one generation so far of young people, have a connection with a work of art. That's huge."

PARRSBORO

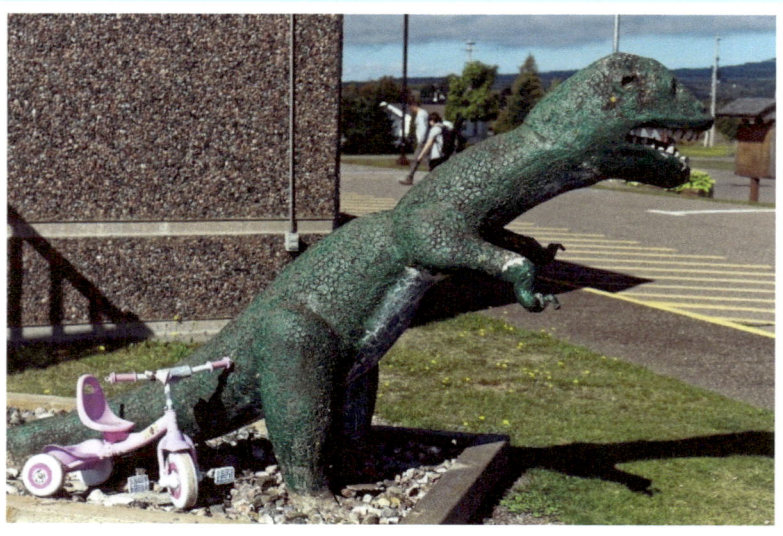

T-REX DEFENDS ROCK, MINERAL AND FOSSIL SHOP

The green statue of a T-Rex stands outside of The Parsboro Rock and Mineral Shop and Museum. This shop was founded in 1948. Elden George, the Fossil Shop's owner, discovered the penny-sized footprints of a Coelophysis dinosaur, which has footprints the size of a penny. This started a frenetic fossil hunting binge in the area that goes on to the present day.

George is a super star in the geological world, because of all the amazing fossil finds that he has made. Also, his shop is the oldest registered rock shop in Canada. Although the building and the sign are unassuming; the museum, fossil finds, and rocks are impressive. Half of the shop is museum and the other half is rocks, tourist souvenirs, sculptures made of natural materials. Parsboro is in the Minas Basin on the Bay of Fundy where some of the highest tides in the world are found.

TURO

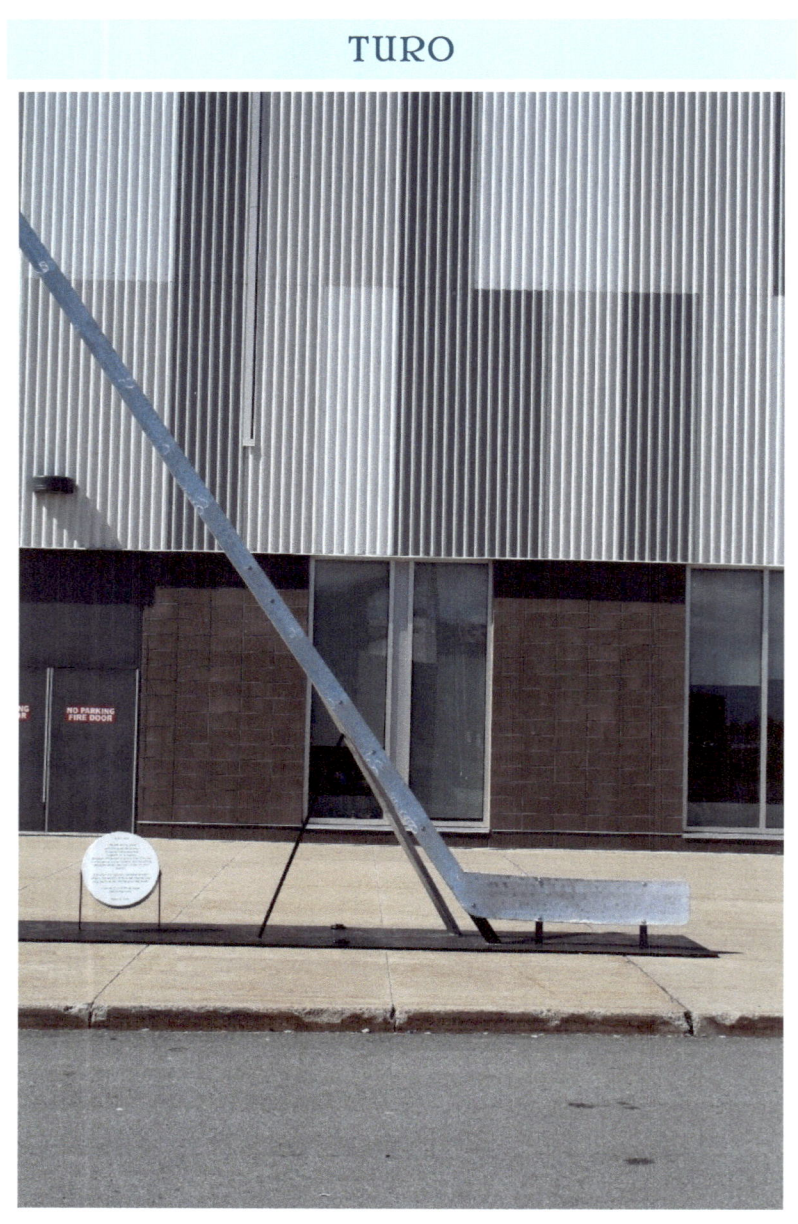

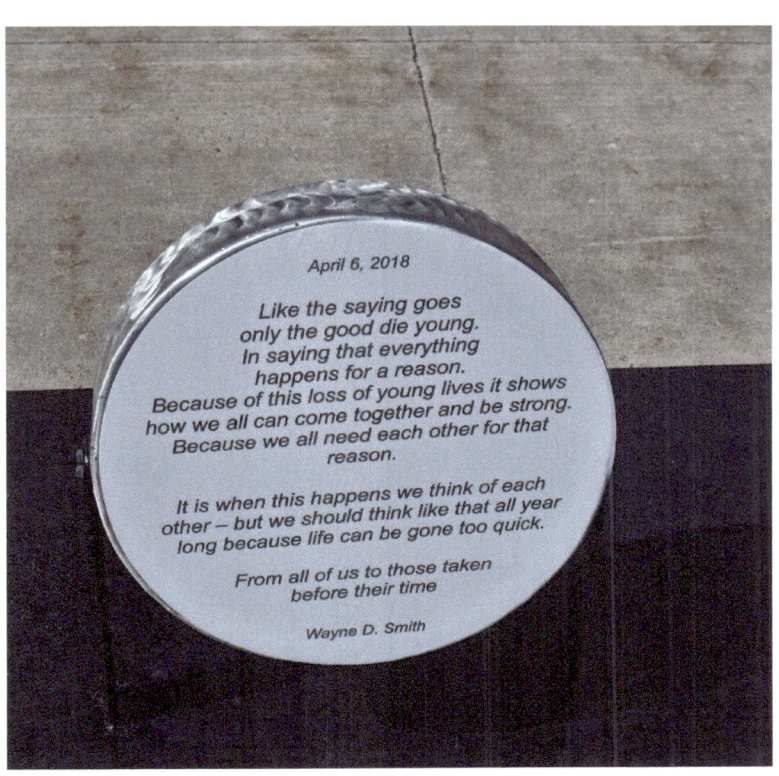

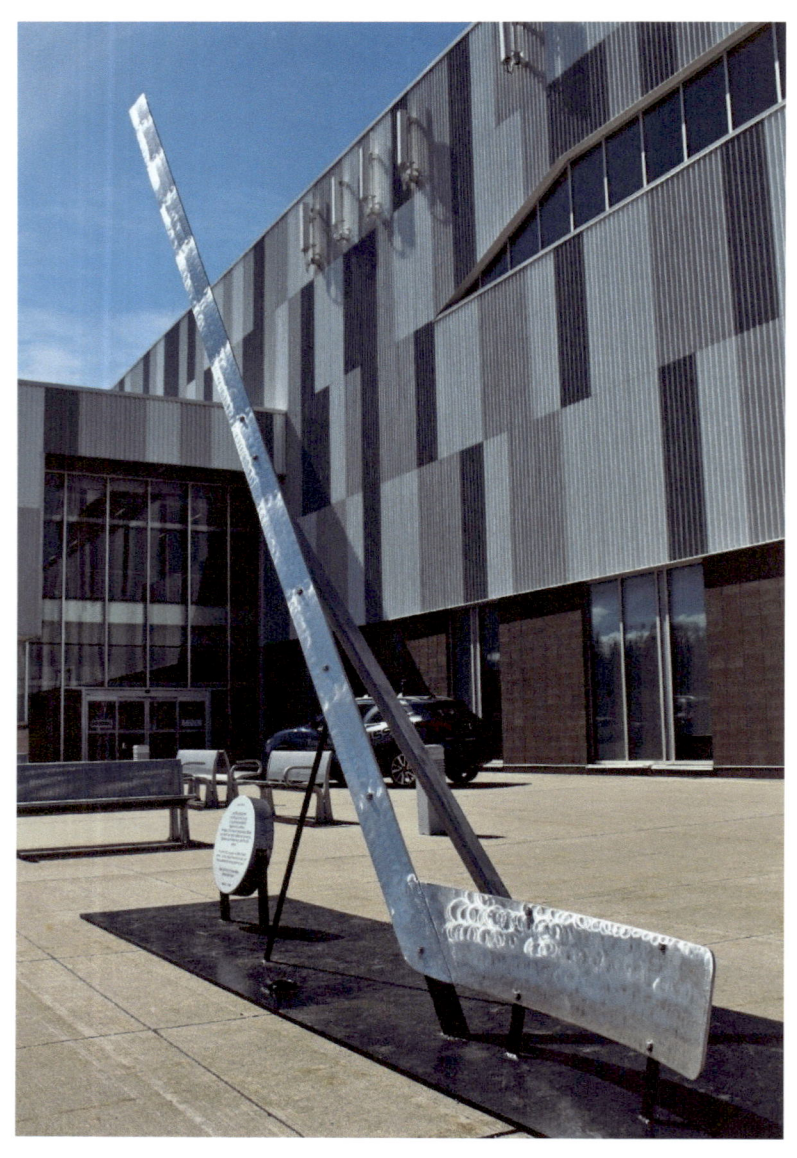

GIANT HOCKEY STICK AS A TRIBUTE

A six-metre tall, aluminum hockey stick stands outside of the Rath Eastlink Community Centre in Truro, Nova Scotia. The artist, Wayne Smith, who is a welder wrote a poem the night that the 16 hockey players from the *Humboldt Broncos* died in a vehicle crash. However, he wanted to do more, so he built a hockey stick that is five times bigger than an ordinary one. Smith comes from Salmon River, Nova Scotia and has built large sculptures before. One of his biggest weighs 25 tonnes. Reactions to the giant hockey stick sometimes gets very emotional, and some of the local hockey players want to have their photos taken near it. Sometime in the future the sculpture will be moved closer to the Community Center's entrance.

PRINCE EDWARD ISLAND

CAPE EGMONT

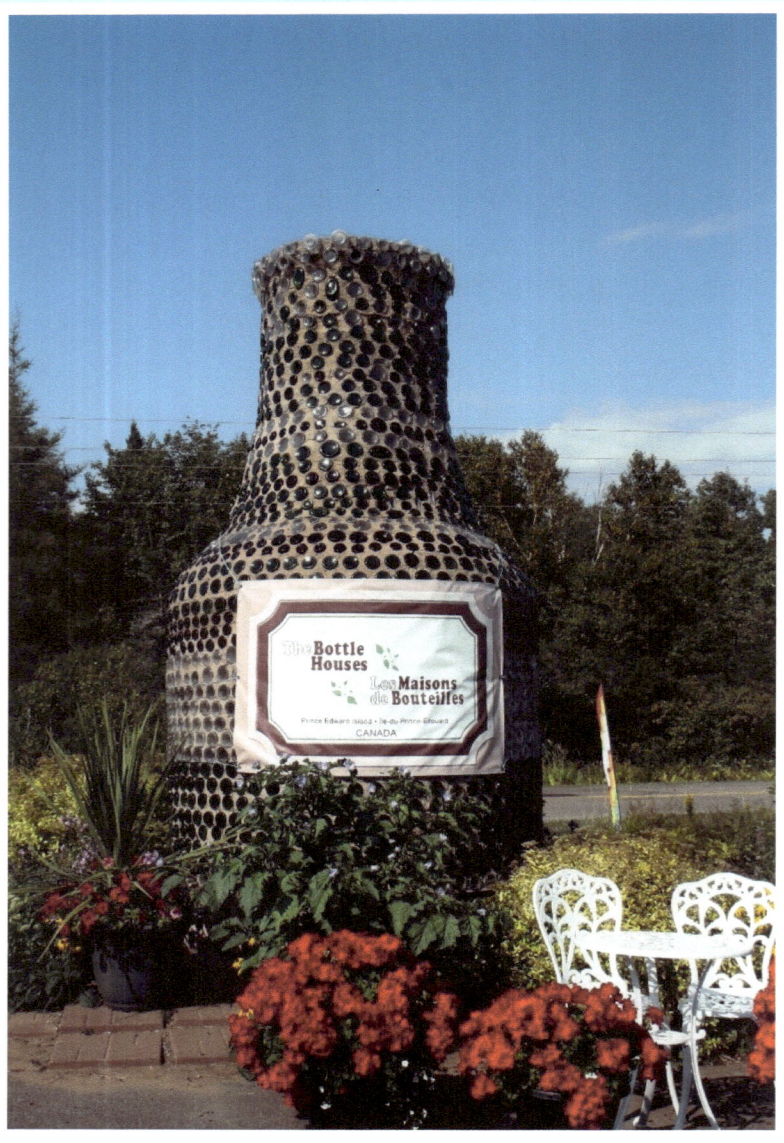

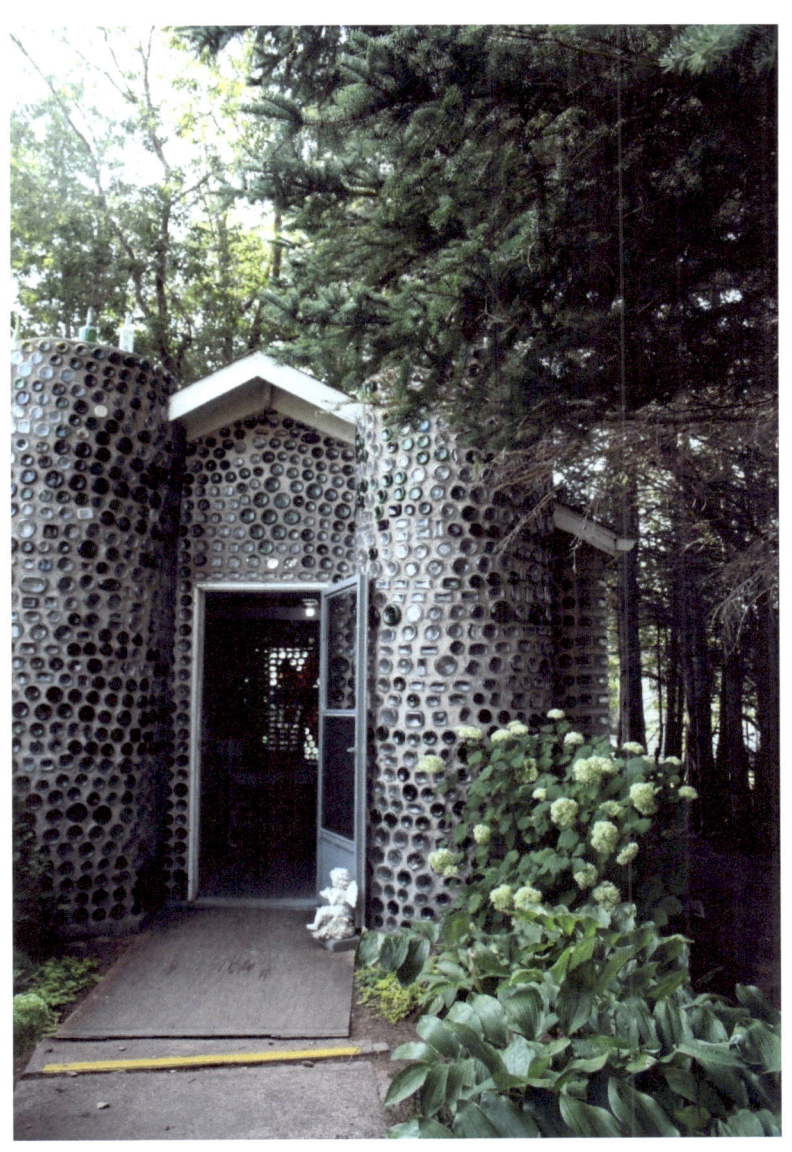

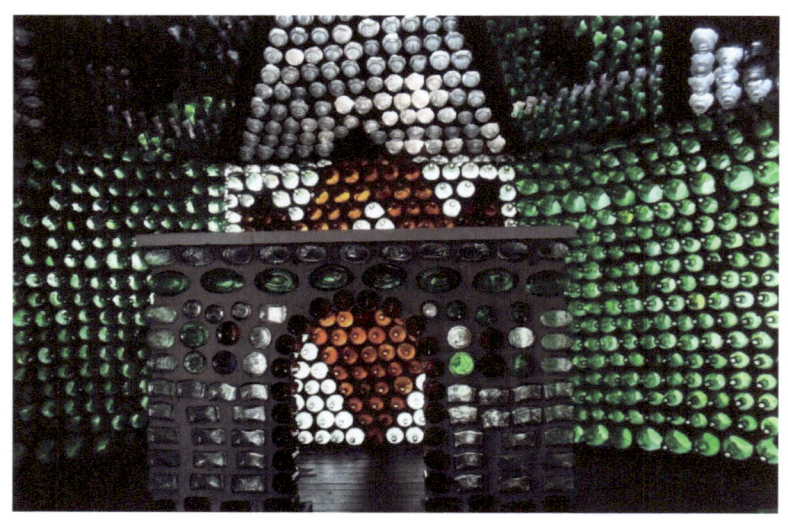

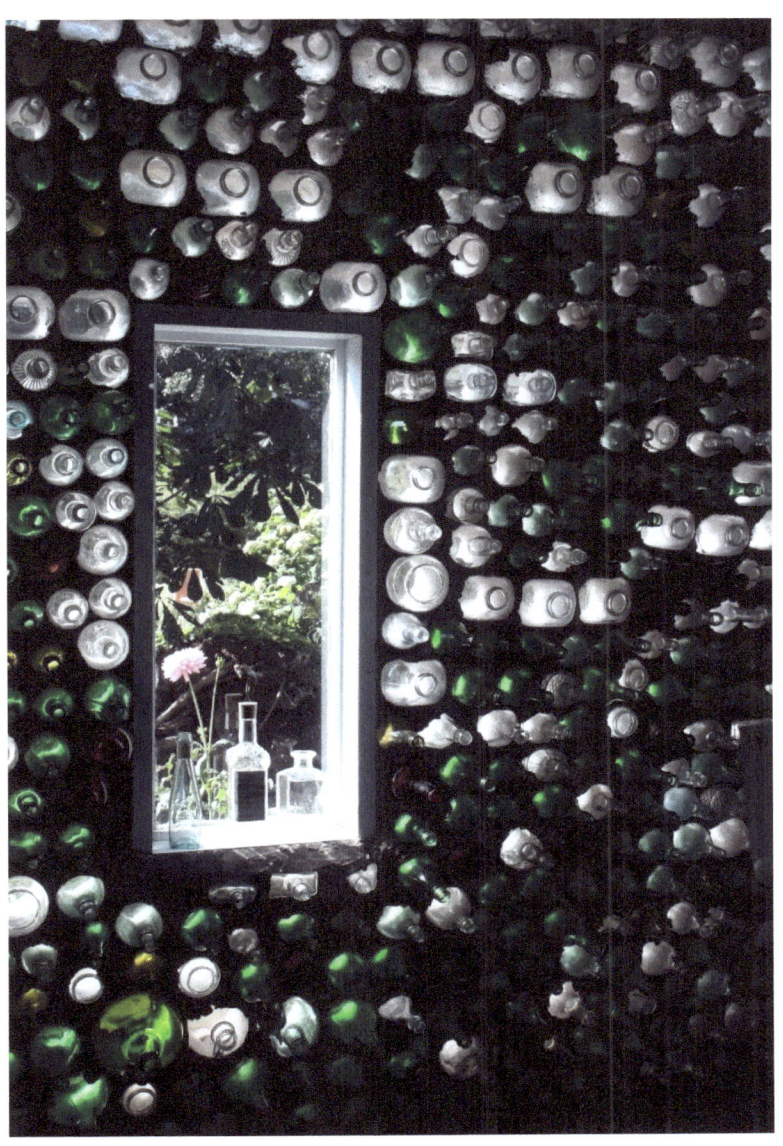

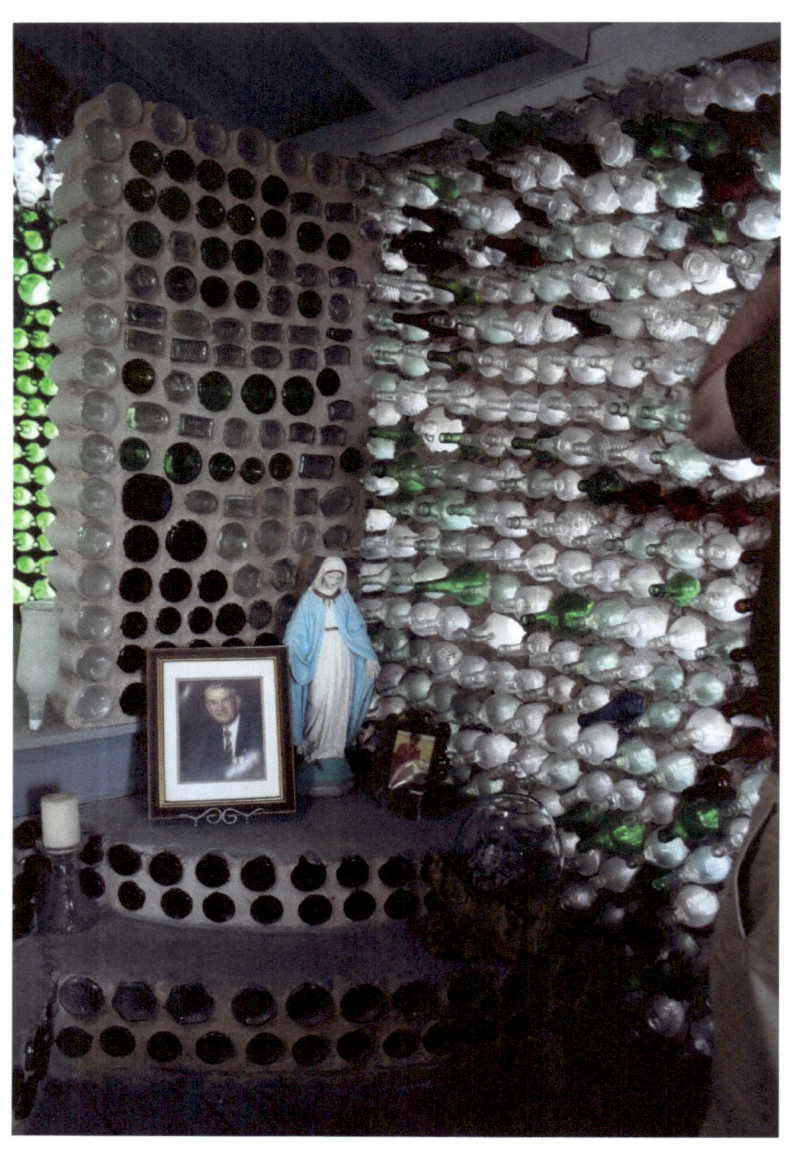

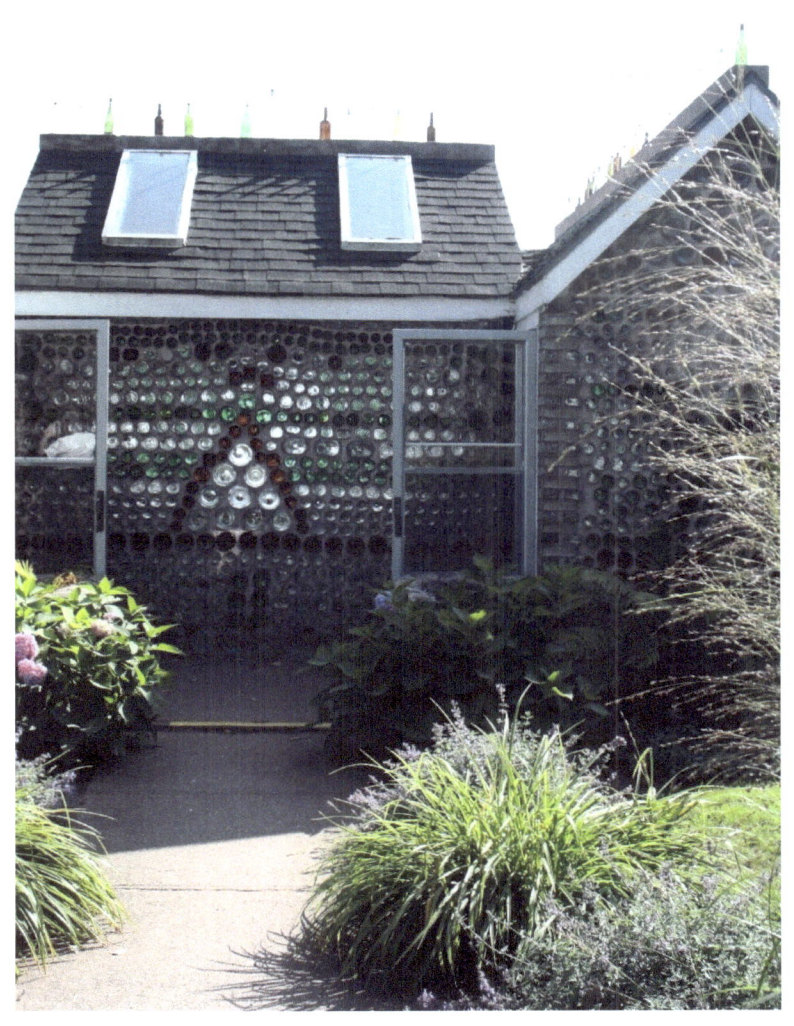

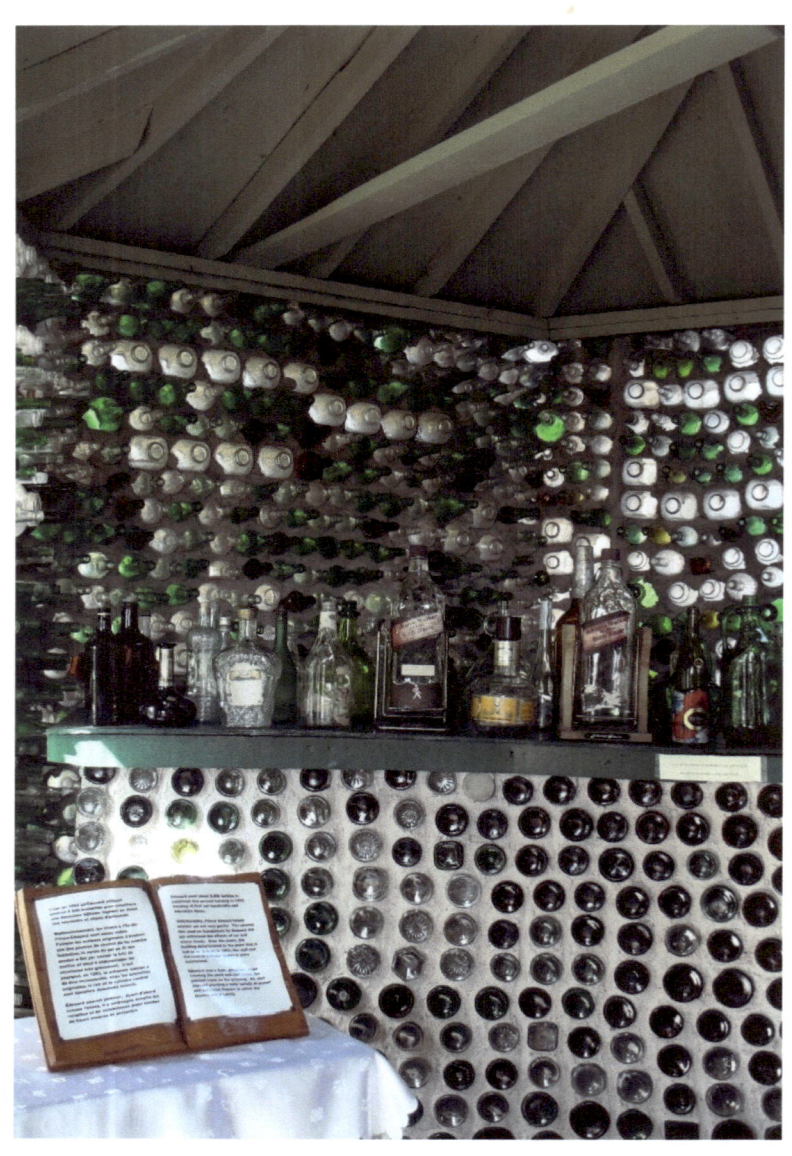

MESSAGE IN A BOTTLE

Edouard Arsenault was born in 1914 and worked as a fisherman, a carpenter, and a lighthouse keeper. In 1979, when he retired at age 66, his dream was to build houses made of bottles. In the beginning he got the glass votive containers that the Catholic churches disregarded. Then he started going around in his old truck collecting bottles from the dance halls, the legion, restaurants, and the dump. [6]

He built a chapel, a six-gabled house, and a tavern using 25,000 bottles that otherwise would have been thrown away.

Arsenault was ahead of his time doing a lot of recycling and repurposing. He showed his spirituality in his stunningly luminous chapel and his Acadian sense of humour in the tavern.

Arsenault also built a giant bottle statue that can be seen in front of the gift shop. The property has beautiful ponds and gardens and attracts a lot of tourists to Cap Egmont, PEI.

---
[6] www.bottlehouses.com

CAVENDISH

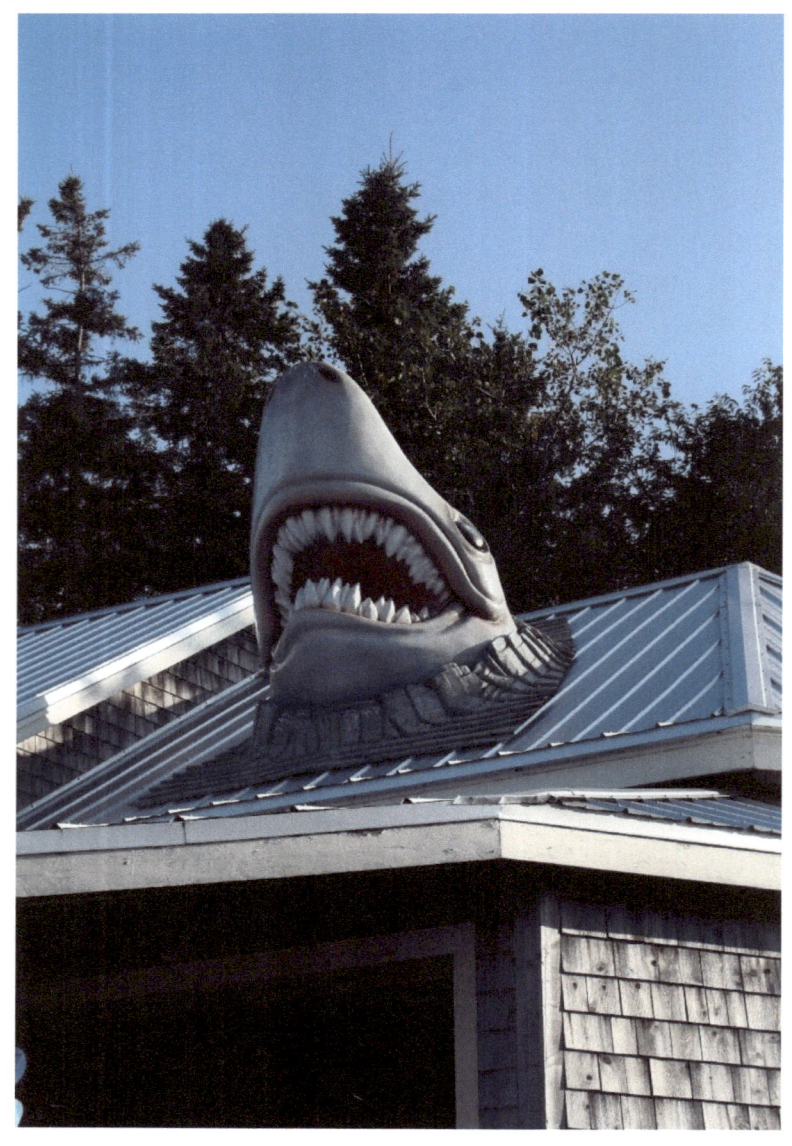

SHARK HEAD ON A ROOF

Above the "Costal Culture" store in Cavendish, PEI, there is a fierce-looking shark head up on the roof. The locals say that there used to be a mixed clothing store there, with an owner nick-named "Sharkie." Even though there is a new owner and a different store the shark head is still displayed. However, no one seems to remember how "Sharkie" got his name.

LAURETTE

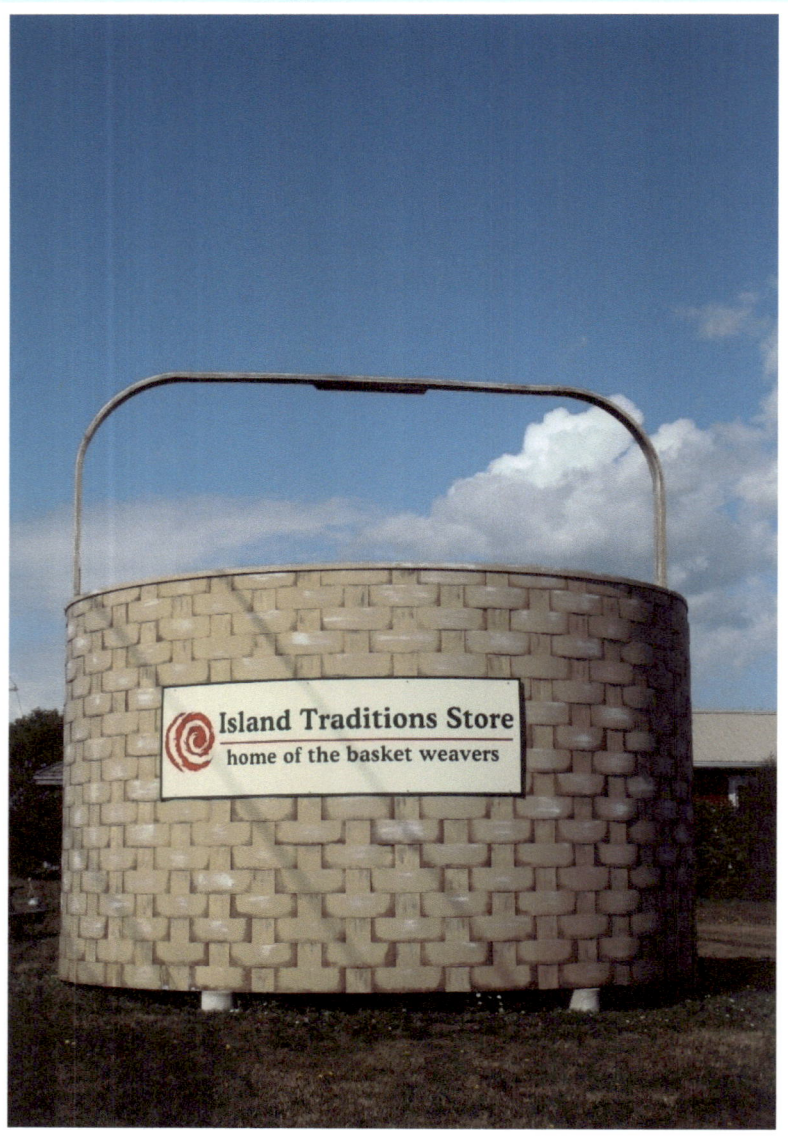

THE LARGEST WOVEN BASKET ON PEI

A giant "woven" basket can be found in Laurette, PEI. It is on the lawn of the *Island Traditions Store* which is home of expert basket weavers. Their advertisement says: "Our basket weavers transform an ash tree into timeless and stunning baskets with hand carved handles and hoops. Sweet grass, tree bark, and roots are incorporated into one of a kind creations. The store also showcases a variety of works by over 100 local accomplished artisans." [7]

The giant basket certainly is a roadside attraction and some of the big stuff in the Maritimes.

---

[7] http://islandtraditionsstore.com/

O'LEARY

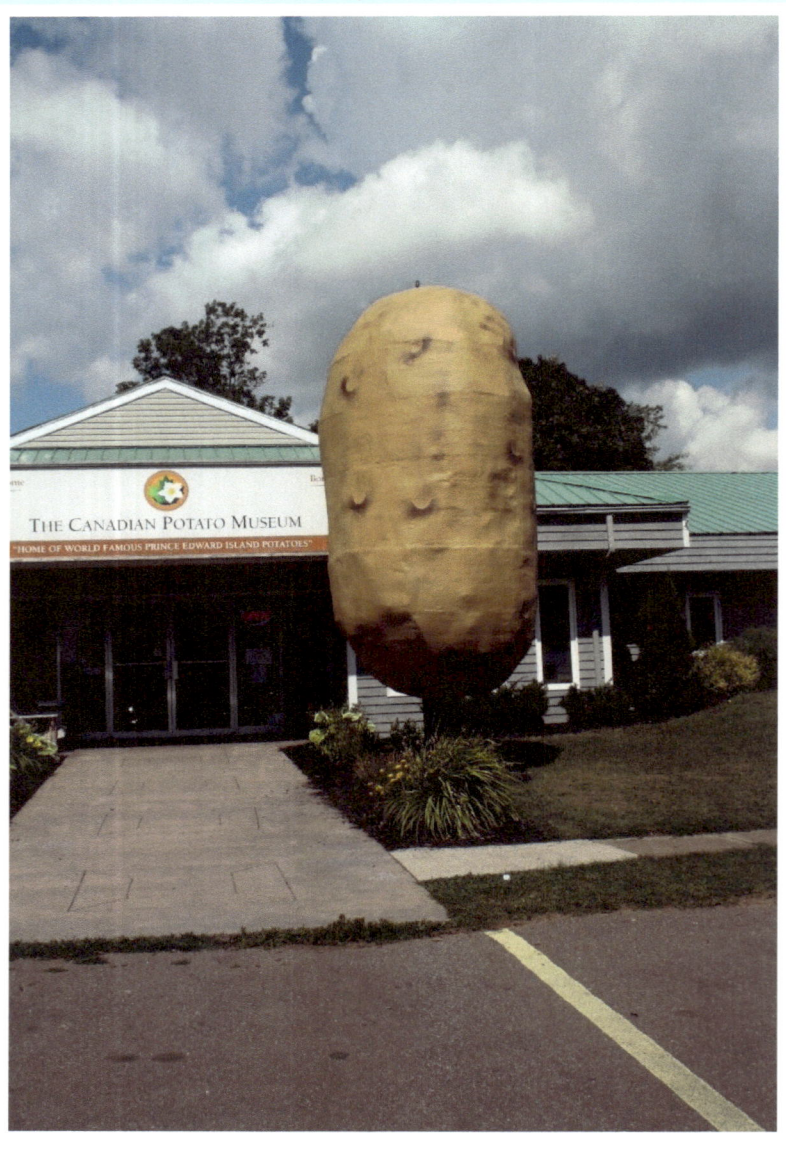

POTATO MUSEUM

The Potato Museum on 1 Dewar Lane, in O'Leary, Prince Edward Island covers 7,000 square feet and has been welcoming guests since 1993. It is the largest museum dedicated to the humble tuber in the world. The popular tourist attraction contains a heritage chapel, a log barn, a little red schoolhouse, and a building containing some antique potato related machinery. Right outside of the front door, there is a massive statue of a potato. Made of fiberglass, it stands 4.3 meters high and is 2.1 meters in diameter.

Some say it is the biggest potato statue around, but there are other rival potatoes that might compete with it. Maugerville, New Brunswick has a giant potato that has been standing for decades and it just might be a little bit bigger?

In any case The Potato Museum captures an important part of Prince Edward Island's heritage. When you first enter the tourist site, you are treated to potato fudge that has real mashed potatoes in it. It just part of the Island's hospitality.

SUMMERSIDE

BERNIE, THE TRAVELLER

Outside of Clark's Sunny Isle Motel is a wooden statue that some have named "Bernie," after the movie "Weekend at Bernie's." The movie was a comedy about a dead man that some friends were trying to pass off as still alive. The motel's statue was carved by a local man named Bill Gallant in 2001. It has a pallor to it, even though the face was painted skin colour.

The owner of the motel, Myles Clark, comments, "In recent years we had a lot of activity around the statue due to the fact that he is now a Poke stop for the *Pokémon Go*® game. People drive up ... sometimes getting out, to recharge or get Poke balls." Bernie has been featured on a local Maritime television station too.

ABOUT KATHERINE E. TAPLEY-MILTON

Katherine Tapley-Milton lives with her husband, Dave, and 6 cats in Sackville, New Brunswick. She graduated from Mount Allison University with a B.A. in the areas of psychology, sociology, and history and then got a 2-year Master of Theological Studies degree from Tyndale Seminary in Willowdale, Ontario in 1981. Katherine has been a freelance writer for over 35 years, and her byline has been in hundreds of periodicals.

She has also written, "The Disappearing Mailboxes of New Brunswick and Nova Scotia," in which she has won a Readers' Favorite 5 Star Review Award. Katherine's other books are available online. In May of 2005, she graduated from the BUILT's Customer Service Representative Course in Moncton, N.B. Her hobbies include cooking, organic gardening, writing, reading historical romances, making crafts, and doing volunteer work at the penitentiary.

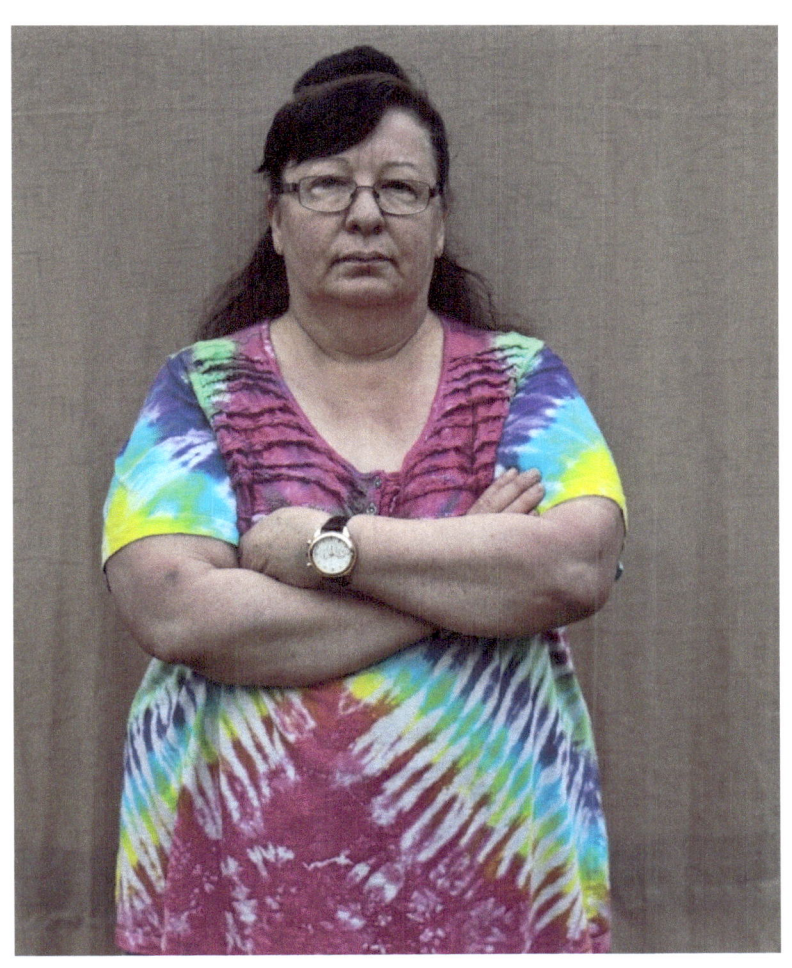

www.ingramcontent.com/pod-product-compliance
Lightning Source LLC
Chambersburg PA
CBHW040235220526
45473CB00001B/251